Power and Poverty in the Church

Power
and
Poverty
in the Church

Yves Congar

Translated by Jennifer Nicholson

Helicon
Baltimore 1964

HELICON PRESS, INC.
1120 N. CALVERT STREET
BALTIMORE, MARYLAND 21202

THIS BOOK WAS FIRST PUBLISHED IN FRANCE BY LES EDITIONS DU CERF,
UNDER THE TITLE *POUR UNE EGLISE SERVANTE ET PAUVRE*.
© TRANSLATION, 1964, GEOFFREY CHAPMAN LTD.

LIBRARY OF CONGRESS CATALOG CARD NUMBER 64-22971

NIHIL OBSTAT: JOANNES M. T. BARTON, S.T.D., L.S.S., CENSOR DEPUTATUS.
IMPRIMATUR: GEORGIUS L. CRAVEN, EPUS. SEBASTOPOLIS, VIC. GEN.
WESTMONASTERII, DIE 1a MAII 1964

THE *NIHIL OBSTAT* AND *IMPRIMATUR* ARE A DECLARATION THAT A
BOOK OR PAMPHLET IS CONSIDERED TO BE FREE FROM DOCTRINAL OR
MORAL ERROR. IT IS NOT IMPLIED THAT THOSE WHO HAVE GRANTED THE
NIHIL OBSTAT AND *IMPRIMATUR* AGREE WITH THE CONTENTS, OPINIONS
OR STATEMENTS EXPRESSED.

MADE AND PRINTED IN GREAT BRITAIN BY CHARLES BIRCHALL & SONS LTD.,
LIVERPOOL & LONDON

*To his Eminence
Cardinal Lercaro,
Archbishop of Bologna,
who has made himself the
spokesman for the Church
of the Poor: in respectful
and filial homage.*

Contents

Power and Poverty in the Church

Foreword

At the request of a number of friends I have brought together in this volume three essays which are in many respects complementary; two have already appeared in print, the third is unpublished.

The first (Part I) appeared in 1962 in the symposium *L'Episcopat et l'Eglise universelle* (*Unam Sanctam*, 39, Ed. du Cerf). It was well received and aroused considerable response. A passage in Pope John XXIII's address to representatives of the Corps Diplomatique on Maundy Thursday, 11 April 1963, is widely quoted nowadays. His words ring of the Gospel:

'It is the spirit that counts more than the gesture; and this lesson does not apply to the leaders of the Church alone: every position of power, every exercise of authority, is a service. The Pope gladly calls himself *Servus servorum Dei*; he is conscious of being, and strives to be, the servant of all. God grant that those who bear the burden of responsibility for the human community may take to heart this last great lesson of Maundy Thursday, and recognize that their authority will be all the more acceptable to their people for being exercised in a spirit of humble service and complete devotion to the welfare of all men.'[1]

[1] *Documentation cath.*, 5 May 1963, col. 585.

I have inserted into the framework of this first study, before its final section, the text of a paper read at an Anglo-French colloquium, in April 1961, at the Abbey of Bec; it was published, with the other papers of the colloquium, in *Problems of Authority* (London and Baltimore, 1962). We see there how through the centuries the hierarchy of the Church has shaped her life by the ideal of service she received, as her law, from the Lord and the apostles. The institution of the hierarchy, with its unbroken history, bears the imprint of time: like houses or furniture, its style has varied. The Church has to a large extent made history, but history has had a hand in the moulding of her features.

The second study is the published version, with notes giving reference to the supporting documents, of a talk given in Rome, in November 1962, during the first session of the Council, to one of the groups of bishops particularly concerned with the great theme of 'the Church of the Poor'—a very international group, under the chairmanship of Cardinal Gerlier, Archbishop of Lyons (Part II). The theme inspired a number of essays.[1] I would not have dared tackle it in itself, not because I had nothing to say on the subject but because I am too well aware of my inadequacy. All I hoped to do was to offer a contribution, however indirect and remote, within the limits of my competence, to the study of the ideological causes underlying certain modes of behaviour or a certain state

[1]Without attempting an exhaustive list, I may mention: Paul Gauthier, *Jésus, l'Eglise et les pauvres. Réflexions nazaréennes pour le Concile*, trans. in *Christ, the Church and the Poor*, Geoffrey Chapman, London 1964. Mgr. Guyot, Bishop of Coutances, Letter for Lent 1963, *Le mystère de la pauvreté dans l'Eglise*; *Riches et pauvres dans l'Eglise ancienne* (texts collected by A. Hamman), Grasset 1962; special number of *Equipes enseignantes*, 2e trimestre 1962-1963.

of things which has to some extent been conditioned by history. It is a fact that at a time when the whole 'mystique' of the Church stresses love of the poor, and even of poverty, when the Church is almost everywhere truly poor, even sometimes in real need, yet she has the appearance of wealth, and (in a word) of privilege, or has pretensions in that direction. This harms both herself and the cause for whose service she was made and which she does truly desire to serve. How has this regrettable appearance come about?

We should have to study many other aspects of things in the light of both history and theology to throw light on the problems thus raised, which many priests find disturbing and even distressing. What is needed is a history and a theology of the Church's temporal state. There are a number of very suggestive studies on this point,[1] but a great deal remains to be said. I should like one day to devote a whole work to this question: to what extent should and can the Church herself, the Church as such, apply to herself the Gospel requirements that tend to be restricted to individual Christians—forgiveness of enemies, turning the other cheek, choosing the ways of poverty, meeting the temptations of the spirit of possession and power, waging war against the flesh, etc? And many other questions would still need to be considered.

History would, I think, be required for their successful treatment. History is a great teacher of truth, especially if we mean by it something more than erudition pure and simple, profitable as this is. What is wanted is an aware-

[1] I would draw attention to: *Inspiration religieuse et Structures temporelles*, Paris, Econ. et Human., and Edit. Ouvrières, 1948; G. Couvreur, *Les Pauvres ont-ils des droits? Recherches sur le vol en cas d'extrême nécessité*, Rome 1961.

ness, in full knowledge of the facts, of the historical dimension which affects everything existing in this world. We are apt to see not only the mystery of the Church, but all ecclesiastical realities (hierarchy, sacraments, etc.) as if they were supratemporal, and for that matter intemporal. That is one of the reasons why we find it so difficult to try to imagine new forms, a new style, for these sacred realities; sometimes we even dismiss the attempt as presumptuous and idle. The episcopate, for example, is an institution of divine and apostolic origin; but historically it has taken more than one form, and it has been lived in very different styles. Because the episcopate, as authority and as sacrament, is always the same, we are inclined to overlook the gulf that separates the leader of a local community in the early Church, a bishop of feudal times, and a twentieth century pastor. The Church and the priesthood are of all time; but they are also the Church of today, the priesthood of today ... Through familiarity with historical forms we can distinguish more clearly the permanence of the essential and the variation of forms; we can locate the absolute and the relative more exactly, and so better remain true to the absolute while we shape the relative to the needs of the time.

At this moment in time, when the whole Church is studying herself in the mirror of the Gospel and taking stock of her adaptability to the needs of the world, I hope that the papers collected here, however incomplete and imperfect, may in their humble way serve the deep Gospel truth that the Second Vatican Council has taken as its underlying theme.

Strasbourg,
12 May 1963   Y.C.

I

The Hierarchy as Service

SCRIPTURAL SOURCES AND HISTORICAL DEVELOPMENT

Introductory Note

The notion that the hierarchy consists essentially in service is a theme that runs all through Christian tradition. Whether in phrases that have become genuine *topoi*, type-formulae of ecclesiastical literature, such as '*praesse, prodesse* (to be at the head, at the service, of');[1] or in what the Germans call *Devotionsformeln*, titles or style—clausulae such as '*Servus servorum Die* (servant of the servants of God');[2] or in the ideology of service for

[1] See my note on '*Quelques expressions traditionnelles du Service chrétien*', in *L'Episcopet et l'Eglise universelle*, op cit. pp. 101-32.

[2] On these clausulae in the language of religion, cf K. Schmitz, *Ursprung u. Geschichte der Devotionsformeln* (KRtl. Abhdlg, 71), Stuttgart, 1913.—St Augustine had already said that the bishop is *Servus servorum Dei*', *Epist.* 217 (*P.L.* 33-378). We find the expression again in St Gregory: cf. H. Grisar, 'Oekiumenischer Patriarch und Diener der Diener Gottes', in *Zeitsch. f. kath. Theol.* 4 (1880), pp. 468 ff.; (historical context of this saying of St Gregory: his opposition to the title of Oecumenical Patriarch which the Patriarch of Constantinople was arrogating); W. Levison, 'Zur Vorgeschichte der Bezeichnung "servus servorus Dei" ', in *Zeitsch. d. Savigny-St. f. Rechtgesch.*, 37. *Kan.Abt.* 6 (1916), pp. 384-6 (use of the word before St Gregory, in particular by St Benedict); H. Delehaye, 'Servus servorum Dei', in *Bulicev Zbornik* . . . , Zagreb 1924, pp. 377-8 (an inscription in the Church of SS John and Paul in Rome, 'Constantinus servus sanctorum', was misread by de Rossi); L. Levillain, 'Servus serv. Dei', in *Le Moyen Age*, 40 (1930), pp. 5-7 (subscription of pontifical acts since St Gregory); E. F. Sutcliffe, 'Servus serv. Dei', in *The Clergy Review*, 6 (1933), pp. 378-86 (to the beginning of the thirteenth century; not confined to the pope); G. Tellenbach, *Libertas, Kirche u. Weltordnung im Zeitalter d. Investiturstreites*, Stuttgart, 1936, pp. 199-201; H. Leclercq, 'Servus servorum Dei', in *Dict. archéol. chrét. et lit.*, vol. XV (1950), col. 1360-3.

the common good, the good of each and all, contained in
the constantly recurring words *utilis, utilitas;*[1] or in
ordination sermons like the fine discourses of St Augustine;[2] or again in the vocabulary introduced by him and
still in general use, which distinguishes between the
potestas, the authority, of Christ and the pure *ministerium*, or service, of the Church;[3] or finally in treatises
more or less expressly devoted to the duties of those
vested with authority[4]—the theme is endlessly affirmed, from the New Testament down to the present
day.

We shall go first to the New Testament to see what
specific conception of authority Jesus handed down to his
disciples and how the apostles understood it; for it is on
that level that we as Christians must seek to understand
and to be 'reformed in the newness of our mind' to the
mind of our Master (Rom. 12:2; Eph. 4:23 [section 1]).
Then we shall sketch in the history of authority in the

[1]See note 1 above.

[2]See the *Serm. tract.* 32 of the *Sermones inediti* published by D. G.
Morin (*Miscell. Agostiniana*, vol I, Rome 1930, pp. 563-75), who
thought it so fine that he edited it before the others: 'Discours inédits
de saint Augustine pour l'ordination d'un évéque', in *Rev. bénéd.* 30
(1913), pp. 393-412, translated in St Augustine, *Le Visage de l'Eglise*,
(*Unam Sanctam*), 31 (Paris 1958, pp. 219-24), and also St Augustine's sermons on the anniversary of his own consecration as bishop,
Serm. 339 and 340 (*P.L.* 38, 1480-4). See also M. Jourjon, 'L'évêque
et le peuple de Dieu selon saint Augustin', in *Saint Augustin parmi
nous*, Le Puy-Paris, 1954, pp. 149-97 (with a translation of Sermons
339 and 340); 'L'évêque comme membre du peuple de Dieu selon
saint Augustin', in *Bull. des. Fac. cath. de Lyon*, N.S. 11 (1952), pp.
21-41; H. Hohensee, *The Augustinian Concept of Authority*, New York,
1954.

[3]See D. Zahringer, *Das kirkliche Priestertum nach dem hl. Augustinus*,
Paderborn, 1931. Cf. especially *Tract. V in Joann.*, 7.

[4]There is a vast literature on 'Mirrors' and *De officiis*, less well-known
when it deals with the clergy than with princes (W. Berges, *Die*

life and thought of the Church (section 2); and finally propound a synthesis and interpretation on general lines (section 3).

Fürstenspiegel d. hohen u. späten Mittelalters, Stuttgart, 1938). The *De consideratione* of St Bernard was widely read and extensively quoted. St Bonaventure expressed his idea of the superior in a less famous work, *De sex aliis Seraphim* (*Opera*, Vol. VIII, pp. 131-51). Cf. Denys the Carthusian, *De vita et regimine praesulum* (*Opera*, Vol. XXXVII pp. 11-57). There have been editions recently of M. Bucer's *Traité de l'amour du prochain* (ed. H. Strohl; cf. pp. 37 ff.), and Dom Claude, Martin's *La Perfection du Chef* (ed. D. Hesbert, 1952). For the many treatises on the ideal of the bishop at the time of the Reformation, cf. P. Broutin, *L'évêque dans la tradition pastorale du XVIe siècle*, Paris, 1953.

For the application of the theme to kings, see A. Dumas, 'Le serment de fidélité et la conception du pouvoir du Ier au IXe siècle', in *Rev. hist. Droit fr. étr.*, 1931, pp. 30-51, 289-321 (pp. 366 ff.); T. Silverstein, 'The Throne of the Emperor Henry in Dante's Paradise and the Medieval Conception of Christian Kingship', in *Harvard Theol. Rev.*, 32 (1939) pp. 115-29.

I

Texts from the Gospels and References in New Testament Literature

Our Lord spoke with exceptional exactness and emphasis on the subject of service. He did so on three occasions. The third was during the celebration of the Last Supper (St John is our witness here, with Luke 22 : 24-7); the first two were at definite and very important moments in his evangelic ministry; our information comes from the Synoptics.

The question of precedence

Jesus's preaching in Galilee met with some success among the people; but he knew that the time was come for him to fulfil another chapter in what was written of him; he had to 'go up' to Jerusalem, be rejected by the elders and by the high priests and the scribes, suffer many things, and enter on his passover of death and resurrection (Mark 8 : 31-3; Matt. 16 : 21-3). Jesus and his disciples were living the brief moment between his preaching in Galilee and the drama that was even then gathering in Judaea. Jesus went to Syro-Phoenicia and to Syria itself,

to Caesarea Philippi. It was there and at that time[1] that
Peter's confession of faith, and the first institution, in
him, of the new ministry to serve the new justice (the
'keys of the kingdom of heaven') took place. Knowing
that he was going to his death, Jesus made provision for
his work to continue in the person of his apostles. From
that time on, says St Matthew (16:21), Jesus set before
the disciples the prospect of the passion, which was at
the same time and by implication the prospect of the
evangelical ministry, or of 'following' in the work of the
holy Gospel (Matt. 16: 24-8; Mark 8: 32-8).

In Judaism the right to first place was a matter for
endless argument: in gatherings for worship, in administration, at meals, the question of precedence constantly
arose.[2] Perhaps in consequence of the promise of the keys
of the kingdom to Peter, the other disciples fell to dis-
puting 'which of them should be the greatest' (Mark 9:
33; Luke 9: 46; Matt., who removes the episode from
Caesarea Philippi, says ; 'the greater in the kingdom of
heaven', 18: 1). Jesus answered them by both word and
deed; he called a little child into their midst, put his
arm round him, and said, 'Whosoever shall humble himself as this little child, he is the greater in the kingdom
of heaven' (Matt. 18: 4). He went on to explain: should
the apostles be received as great, in their capacity as
apostles and by reason of their ministry, it would have
nothing to do with any greatness of their own, but would
be by reason of Jesus himself, because of his name. Even

---

[1]According to Matt. 16: 13 f.

[2]See the comment of A. Schlatter (*Matthäus*, p. 543), quoted by
W. Grundmann, art. *megas* in, *Theologisches Wörterbuch zum Neuen
Testament* (hereafter referred to as *T.W.N.T.*) vol. IV, p. 538.

a little child bears this same honour, if he is received because of Jesus. Jesus himself has this honour only by reason of the mission he received from his Father. The Father alone is the principle without a source. All comes from him, all is called to return to him.

We must turn to St John for further development of our Lord's meaning. We shall find there Jesus's infinitely far-reaching statements on his glory (the glory which he has given his disciples too: John 17: 22). This is not the glory of a reputation that exalts us in the eyes of men but a glory that Jesus has from the Father, by virture of the fact that he reveals both the condescension and the power of the Father, because he knows no other aim in life than to obey the Father's will and accomplish the design for which the Father sent him.[1] That is why Jesus begins to manifest his glory when he begins his ministry (John 2: 11). That is why he recognizes and proclaims the special time of his glorification as, more than any other, the beginning of his passion, which clearly cannot be separated from the resurrection which followed it: cf. John 7: 39; 12:23-8; 13: 31 ff.; 17: 1 and 5. This is the supreme moment of his obedience to the Father who sent him to seek, amid the dust and thorns, that which was lost.

In this mission, Jesus is filled with the power of God; the Father has given all things into his hand (John 3: 35). 'You call me Master, and Lord. And you say well; for so I am' (John 13: 13). Jesus's authority with regard to the world and men, is absolute, but it is an authority

[1]On this glory *which is from God* (not from men), cf. John 5: 39-44; 7: 16-18; 8: 54. Christ's glory is the glory befitting an only-begotten son: 1: 14. See A. M. Ramsey, *The Glory of God and the Transfiguration of Christ*, London, 1949, pp. 64 ff.

(1) wholly directed to their salvation, by the path of the
deepest humiliation; (2) wholly received from the Father,
depending on him, and constantly referred to him by
Jesus's acknowledgement that he has nothing save from
the Father: Jesus's doctrine is not *his* doctrine, his
judgment is not *his* judgment: cf. John 7: 16; 5: 30;
12: 49, etc.

Who shall have first place?

And now the second episode. Jesus has again announced, 'We go up to Jerusalem' (Mark 10: 33), and
intimated that his Messiahship is now to be decisively
affirmed. James and John (Mark 10: 35), or their mother
(Matt. 20: 20), come up to him with a direct, outright
request which must have been in their minds for some
time: that in the kingdom which Jesus is obviously
about to establish, they shall receive the two first and
best places, and sit one on his right hand and the other
on his left. Then the Lord gives a most definitely worded
answer:

'You know that they who seem to rule over the
Gentiles lord it over them: and their princes have
power over them. But it is not so among you; but whosoever will be greater shall be your minister; and
whoever will be first among you shall be the servant
of all. For the Son of man also is not come to be ministered
unto, but to minister and to give his life as a redemption
for many' (Mark 10: 42-5; Matt. 20: 25-8).

He uses terms of great force. In the Gospel order, as
in the order of earthly societies, the great and the first
do exist. In earthly societies they make their power felt,

they bear themselves as masters;[1] the whole relationship of inequality between others and themselves is a relationship of subjection on the one hand, of mastery on the other. The path that, according to the Gospel, leads to the rank of *first* or *great* is quite different, even the exact opposite. It lies in seeking a situation or relationship not of power but of service, of *diakonos*, servant, or *doulos*, slave, common workman. These two terms lie at the very heart of the categories which serve to define Christian existence.[2] *Diakonia*, ministry, the position, behaviour and activity of a servant, appears throughout the whole of the New Testament to be as it were coextensive and practically identical with the character of disciple— a man possessed by Christ and living in subjection to him. The title *doulos*, slave, servant (of God), which had no religious significance in the pagan world, best expresses this complete belonging to Christ, in which we become also the servants of all our brothers. The attitude of service, not of power, which Jesus makes his

[1]The verb *kurieuo* means: to be or become a lord, to act as a lord, to play the lord. *Katakurieuo* (cf. 1 Peter 5: 3) adds to *kurieuo* a sense of making one's power felt, exercising dominion to one's own profit even to the detriment of others; cf. W. Foerster, in *T.W.N.T.* vol. III, pp. 1097-8 (trans. H. P. Kingdom, as *Lord* [1958]). The word *katexousiazousin* by itself means no more than 'to exercise power' (over one's subjects), but no doubt has here a similar nuance of dominion (*ibid.* II, p. 572). Cf. 3 John 9, on Diotrephes, who loved to have the pre-eminence, *philoproteuon*.

[2]See articles *diakoneo*, *diakonia*, *diakonos* (H. W. Beyer) and *duolos* (K. H. Rengstorf) in *T.W.N.T.* vol III pp. 81-93 and 264-83. Catholic authors: L. Deimel *Leib Christi* . . . , Freiburg, 1940, pp. 65 ff., 89 ff., 119 ff.; E. Walter, *Diener des Neuen Bundes. Das Priestertum d. kathol. Kirche*, Paderborn, 1940; J. Colson, *La fonction diaconale aux origines de l'Eglise*, Paris, 1960. Protestant authors: W. Brandt, *Dienst und Dienen im Neuen Testament*, Gutersloh, 1931; H. Asmussen, *Die Kirche und das Amt*, Munich, 1939, pp. 188 ff.; *Das diakonische Amt der Kirche*, ed. H. Krimm, Stuttgart, 1953.

disciples' law, he expressly links with his own—the Master's—for the disciple is not merely a pupil under instruction; he imitates the master and shares his life.[1] Jesus lived his mission, and defined it in terms of the Isaian Servant.[2] He came not to 'domineer', not to exact service, but to serve as a slave and even to live as a slave, to the point of actually being sold, of letting himself be the equivalent of a ransom.[3] Because their life belongs wholly to Christ, is wholly of him and for him, the disciples can rise only by humbling themselves, only by following Christ on the downward path of self-giving and self-abnegation, along which St Paul has traced God's victorious trajectory to the death of the cross and from the tomb to glory.

From the form of God to the form of a servant

The wonderful passage of Philippians 2: 6-11, which

[1]See K. H. Rengstorf, art. *mathetes*, in *T.W.N.T.* vol. IV, pp. 417-65.

[2]Cf. Isaias 42: 1 and the note in *Bible de Jérusalem* on this text.

[3]In his commentary on Matt. 20: 25-8, Thomas Aquinas, whose roots in the Gospel becomes more apparent the better one knows him, propounds an example to himself: Can Christ, who allowed himself to be served (cf. Matt. 4: 11; John 12: 2), himself be called *servus*? His answer is: Yes, for 'servus dicitur qui accipitur in pretium: et ipse fecit se pretium et dedit se redemptionem pro multis . . . ' Cf. the Office of the Holy Sacrament, *Pange lingua* ('quem in mundi pretium . . . '); *Verbum supernum* ('Se nascens dedit socium . . . se moriens in pretium . . . ').

Cf. St Bernard; in his comment on the theme of service by the angels, who exercise a pure *ministerium* for our benefit, he adds that Christ serves us by giving himself to us: 'Non sic minister ille sublimior cunctis, sed et humilior universis, qui semetipsum obtulit sacrificium laudis, qui Patri offerens animam suam, nobis ministrat usque hodie carnem suam' (*Sermo* 1 *in Festo S. Michaelis*, n. 3, *P.L.* 183, 449).

may have been a Christian hymn, must be read in the
same light as the sayings we have already quoted: the
way of the flesh is opposed to the way of the spirit, the
way of the world to the way of the Gospel:

'Christ Jesus, who, though he was in the form of God,
did not count equality with God a thing to be grasped,
but emptied himself, taking the form of a servant,
being born in the likeness of men.
And being found in human form he humbled himself
and became obedient unto death, even death on a
cross.
Therefore God has highly exalted him and bestowed
on him the name which is above every name,
that at the name of Jesus every knee should bow,
in heaven and on earth and under the earth, and
every tongue confess that Jesus Christ is Lord, to the
glory of God.'

(Translation, Revised Standard Version)

The text speaks only of Christ, but exegetes are in
general agreed in seeing here an allusion to the first
Adam, from whom our carnal man proceeds.[1] Though

[1]For this interpretation of Phil. 2: 6-11, see the Protestant exegetes:
J. Héring, already in 1936 (*Rev. Hist. Phil. rel.*, pp. 196 ff.); O. Cull-
mann (*The Christology of the New Testament*, trans. S. C. Guthrie and
C. A. M. Hall, London 1959, pp. 166 ff.); Bo Reicke. Catholic exe-
getes: L. Bouyer, 'Harpagmos', in *Rech. sc. rel.*, 39 (1951—*Mél. J.
Lebreton*, 1), pp. 281-8; J. Schmitt, D. Barthélémy, etc.

The Eastern *Anaphoras* (St Basil, St Gregory of Nazianzus, Theo-
dore of Mopsuestia, John of Bosra) and the *Catechesis* of the Greek
Fathers (cf. my paper quoted below, n. 2 p. 30) see in Phil. 2:6-11, the
summary of the mystery of the Incarnation which, being redemptive,
is essentially '*kenosis*'. That St John's view of the mystery of Christ
was fundamentally similar appears from O. Prunet, *La Morale
crétienne d'après les écrits johanniques*, Paris, 1957. p. 42; cf. pp. 71, 124-5.

existing in the form of man, that is as creature and
servant, Adam desired and still does desire to enjoy a
form of God, which he understands as independence and
self-affirmation limited by nothing and no one: 'You
shall be as Gods, knowing' (that is, yourselves determin-
ing) 'good and evil' (Gen. 3: 5 and 22). But desiring to
be as God, Adam descended into a state of nakedness
(Gen. 3: 11), a life of toil and attachment to the senses.
Man is never his own master; he is always under
domination. If he breaks away from the domination of
God, he falls under the domination of the 'Powers'....
But though Christ existed in the form of God, he did not
bear himself possessively; he did not cling to the divine
form as men cling to a prize; he took on himself the form
of a slave, our form. And even in this form in which,
being God, he could *by right* have claimed to reign
supreme over the world, he did not demand his right
possessively, he did not snatch it or lay covetous claim
to it; he was pleased to obtain it from God by humble,
crucifying service, abasing himself in the spirit of love.
... That is why, while Adam fell through his desire to
exalt himself, Christ received the Name above all names,
the name of the First absolutely, the name of 'Lord', at
which every knee bows on earth, in heaven, and in hell.
'Whosoever shall exalt himself shall be humbled; and he
that shall humble himself shall be exalted' (Matt. 23: 12
and parallels—read from v. 8; Luke 14:11; 18: 14, and
2: 48-52).

The way of love in humility and service

The 'first' man within us longs to dominate, to play
the master. . . . Christ came as the 'second Adam'

or rather, as St Paul says, the 'last Adam', the final Adam, eschatological man (*eschatos Adam*: 1 Cor. 15: 45): not a man of domination, but a man of obedience, giving thanks, a man in communion with others, complying with others, or rather complying and communing with God in them, a man of God, who is 'all in all' (1 Cor. 15: 28). The first Adam has life, 'was made into a living soul' (Gen. 2: 7; 1 Cor. 15: 45). He lives but his life constantly wastes away and renews itself by devouring, that is destroying, other creatures, appropriating them to itself. . . . But normal life, *true* life, should not be sustained by bringing death. Life should come from within and communicate life. 'The last Adam is a quickening spirit' (1 Cor. 15: 45). He rediscovers the logic of the spirit, which is not to feed on what it brings in to itself from without and destroys but to shine out from within. This can be achieved only when the order of obedience is perfectly fulfilled,[1] when everything is brought back to its Principle, when 'God' is 'all in all'. It will be, it is, achieved *by Christ*: 'As in Adam all die, so also in Christ all shall be made alive' (1 Cor. 15: 22). But Christ will achieve this in the end only because he has been like this from the beginning of his mortal life in the flesh. The way resembles its end, and only thus can it lead to its end (cf. John 14: 1-11). The Father is already in Jesus. The way leading to God who is 'all in all', leading that is to mankind in communion, is a state where others are not destroyed to sustain life, but where life, coming from

[1]Cf. 1 Cor. 15: 23-8: 'Every one in his own order; the first-fruits, Christ; then they that are of Christ, who have believed in his coming . . . He must reign, until he hath put all his enemies under his feet . . . And, when all things shall be subdued unto him, then the Son also himself shall be subject unto him that put all things under him, that God may be all in all.'

God, shines out on all men; it is the way of love in humble service. 'For you, brethren, have been called unto liberty. Only make not liberty an occasion to the flesh; but by charity of the spirit serve one another. For all the law is fulfilled in one word: *Thou shalt love thy neighbour as thyself*. But if you bite and devour one another, take heed you be not consumed one of another' (Gal. 5: 13-15): all the rest of the chapter should be read in this light. The spirit of possessiveness destroys; *agape*, love, which is poured forth within us by the Holy Spirit (Romans 5: 5), shines forth and edifies (1 Cor. 8: 1, and the whole of chapter 13).

Such is the way of Christ. Such is first of all the way of 'God', that is, of the Father: 'Be ye therefore followers of God (that is, of the Father), as most dear children; and walk in love (*agape*), as Christ also hath loved us and hath delivered himself for us. . . .' (Eph. 5: 1-2, and cf. 25). Holy Scripture leaves us in no doubt that the impulse of humble, serving, self-sacrificing love begins in 'God', that is in the bosom of the Father. 'God indeed was in Christ, reconciling the world to himself.'[1] The 'self-annihilation' of the Son follows the Father's stripping of himself. If Jesus reveals the Father ('Philip, he that seeth me seeth the Father also'), we can go so far as to say that he reveals in the Father a possibility of Grace, even a disposition towards *being* Grace, and so coming to us, stooping down to us, humbling himself: because he *is* Love.[2] We should not be talking of the

---

[1] 2 Cor. 5: 19.   Cf. John 3: 16; 1 John 4: 10.

[2] See 'Dum visibiliter Deum cognoscimus', in *Les Voies du Dieu vivant*, Paris, 1962, pp. 79-108. On the sacrifice of God, cf. Y. Congar, *Lay People in the Church*, London, pp. 149 ff. J. Rivière, 'Le sacrifice du Père dans la Rédemption d'après saint Ambroise' in *Rev. Sc. rel.*, 1939, pp. 1-23, sees this as a purely literary idea, not a theological

God we know in Jesus Christ if we stopped short at the idea that he is the 'Prime Mover, himself unmoved' (Aristotle), or that he is the One who loves himself (Plotinus). In Jesus Christ, God has revealed himself leaning towards us, bending over us, the Love-Gift, Grace. . . .

'If I have washed your feet . . .'

We come to know the Father through what is supremely manifested in the attitude of the Son, *come down from Heaven* (John 1: 18; 3: 11 and 16; 14: 1-11; 17: 6):

> 'After he had washed their feet, he said to them: Know you what I have done to you? You call me Master and Lord. And you say well; for so I am. If then I, being your Lord and Master, have washed your feet; you also ought to wash one another's feet. For I have given you an example, that as I have done to you, so you do also. Amen, amen, I say to you: The servant is not greater than his lord; neither is the apostle greater than he that sent him. If you know these things, you shall be blessed if you do them' (John 13: 12-17).

The Lord's order here—we might almost say, his ordination—comes in the long series of passages in which St John's Gospel expresses the idea of mission flowing, as it were cascading, from the Father to the incarnate Son and from the incarnate Son to the apostles

one. The Lutheran theologians G. Aulén (*Christus Victor*, trans. A. G. Herbert, London, 1931) and A. Nygren (*Agape and Eros*, trans. P. S. Watson, London, 1953) are not entirely free from exaggeration and unilateralism, but are worth reading on this point.

and the Church.[1] God's design is in fact to communicate himself (cf 1 John: 1-3). For this the reality on high must, through successive stages, exist here below in a form which shares its virtue though never in full and sovereign measure, and mirrors the behaviour of its source and reality. The Father has sanctified the Son and sent him to the world (John 10: 36). The Son in turn has sanctified and purified the apostles, and consecrates them by sending them to the world (cf John 17: 14, 17-19). This is the moment of their consecration. The synoptic Gospels give us the account of the institution of the Eucharist at this point. St John omits it, substituting the washing of feet, which he alone reports. Corresponding to 'Do this for a commemoration of me', we have here, 'As I have done to you, so do also'. The ordination of the apostles is an ordination in terms of service. Christ who washes the disciples' feet and speaks of his action in this way is the same Christ who knows that the Father has given all things into his hands (13: 3) and who expressly recalls his character of Master and Lord, *Didaskalos* and *Kurios*, just as he refers to his *exousia*, his power, at his final sending of the apostles

[1] There are correspondences and connections between 'As the Father hath sent me, I also send you' (John 20: 19 f., although the verbs used are not the same, cf. 4: 38; 17: 17-19), 'As the Father hath loved me, I also have loved you' (17: 18 and 25; 13: 34; 15: 9), the communication of the knowledge of the Father to the Son and from the Son to the disciples, with the 'I know (my sheep) and (my sheep) know me, as the Father knoweth me and I know the Father' (10: 14-15), the glorification of the Father in the Son (13: 31; 14: 13), then of the Son, and so of the Father (15: 8) in those he sends (17: 1-5 and 6, 8, 10), the mutual presence of the Father and the Son, of the Son and his disciples (14: 20; 15: 4), etc. On this theme of communication, see R. Bréchet, 'Du Christ à l'Eglise. Le dynamisme de l'Incarnation dans l'Evangile selon saint Jean', in *Divus Thomas*, 56 (1953), pp. 67-98.

(Matt. 28: 18). At this supreme moment of the Last
Supper, he repeats his essential teaching: his disciples,
and most especially Simon Peter, are to follow him in
serving one another:

> 'The kings of the Gentiles lord it over them; and
> they that have power over them are called beneficent.
> But you are not so; but he that is the greater among
> you, let him become as the younger; and he that is the
> leader, as he that serveth....' (Luke 22: 25-6.)

'Ourselves your servants!'

We find the echo of the Master's teaching in the
apostles themselves. The first Christian texts are prob-
ably St Paul's. Paul took to himself, as though by right,
the character of *doulos*, slave, in which God manifested
himself and gave himself to us.[1] So also do Peter, James
and Jude.[2] Every minister of the Gospel, every Christian, is a *doulos*, a servant of God, of Jesus Christ and
of his brethren.[3] For Jesus's sake Paul, following his
Master, made himself the servant of the faithful and of
all men: 'For we preach not ourselves, but Jesus Christ
our Lord, and ourselves your servants through Jesus' (2
Cor. 4: 5; cf. 1 Cor. 9: 19). Paul has no intention of
'exercising dominion', 'domineering' (2 Cor. 1: 23, the
verb *kurieuo*, cf. above, p. 25, note 1. It is the Lord,
not Paul, who enables the faithful to live in the religious

---

[1]Romans 1: 1; Phil. 1: 1; Gal. 1: 1; Titus 1: 1. Servant of the
faithful: 2 Cor. 4: 5; 1 Cor. 9: 19. Cf. for Epaphras, Col. 4: 12;
for Timothy, 2 Tim. 2: 24.

[2]James 1: 1; 2 Peter 1: 1; Jude 1.

[3]See Rom. 6: 22; 1 Peter 2: 16; Apoc. 1: 1; 2: 20; 7: 3; 19: 2 and
5; 22: 3 and 6.

2

relationship of faith. In the same vein Peter exhorts the elders not to 'lord it' over the flock (1 Peter 5: 3; verb *katakurieuo*).

This position in relation to Christ and—because of and following Christ—in relation to the faithful, entails for St Paul a very significant and also very conscious manner of behaviour. Paul was well able to claim not only his title of apostle, which he always traces back to 'God' (cf. Galatians), but also his apostolic *authority*.[1] Usually, however, he prefers to take his stand—and tells us so—on the spiritual gifts he has received (1 Cor. 7: 40; 2 Cor. 10: 7-8; 11: 5 f., 23 f.; 12: 1-15), on the signs with which God himself is at work, by blessing his servant's labours (2 Cor. 3: 1-3), on his love and devotion (1 Thess. 2: 7-12, a passage to be read in its entirety; Philemon 8-9),[2] and finally on his weakness, for God is pleased to act through this too (2 Cor. 11: 30; 12: 5 and 9). He refrains from claiming or bringing forward the *rights* which he possesses and is concerned only with the exercise of his duties, in a life entirely devoted to service, preferring to give than to receive.[3] He ceaselessly bases his injunctions not on his own authority, which could enforce them, but on the example and behaviour of the Lord; and the whole Christian ethic consists in

[1]See 1 Cor. 7: 10, 12 and 17; 2 Cor. 10: 8; 2 Thess. 3: 9; Philemon 8.

[2]*Ibid.*

[3]Cf. the *Epistle of Barnabas*: 'I will shew you a few things, not as a teacher but as one of yourselves, whereby you shall rejoice in the present circumstances (I, 8); And this also I ask you, as being one of yourselves, and loving you individually and all together above my own life . . . (IV, 6); And though wishing to write much, I am anxious to write not as a teacher but as your devoted slave (IV, 9)' (trans. *S.P.C.K. Texts for Students*, No. 14a, London, 1923).

imitating, or rather continuing, this example.[1] And as
Paul was the first to set himself this task, so he in turn
becomes a model to be followed.[2]

Fundamentally, to have appealed to rights or
authority, even though these were received from the
Lord, would have brought in an element of *self*. Paul's
desire was to be entirely and always in the stream of
grace, grace which suffices (2 Cor. 12: 9), which gives
everything, without cease, in which we find ourselves
at ease only when we ourselves *give* without reserva-
tion. All St Paul's solutions in the realm of what was
later called 'casuistry' are dictated by these ideas, and
in the last resort by the law of *agape* which rules them,
directly from their source in the bosom of the Father,
whose own attribute is love (2 Cor. 13, 13).[3]

The master exacts service. The servant who is a servant 'for the sake of Jesus' *gives*, gives even *himself*.
This too is the difference between the hireling and the
good shepherd (John 10: 10 f.). In one way or another
the conduct of the Christian, and especially the apostolate, because they lie in the realm of *agape*, of self-
giving love, self-sacrificing love, pledge the Christian
and especially the apostle to sacrifice, and ultimately to
the surrender of life itself. Each time Jesus spoke of his
Passion he went on to apply it to the disciples; even thus

[1]Cf. 1 Cor. 9, especially v. 15; 2 Cor. 7: 2 ff.; 2 Thess. 2: 7. Cf.
2 Cor. 9: 7 and Acts 20: 35 (the well-known agraphon: 'It is a more
blessed thing to give, rather than to receive').
[2]Cf. 2 Thess. 3: 7-9; cf. 1 Peter 5: 3 ('a pattern of the flock').
[3]See my paper, 'La Casuistique de saint Paul', in *Sacerdoce et
laïcat devant leurs tâches d'évangelisation et de civilisation*, Paris, 1962, pp.
65-90.

far must they follow their Master.[1] The trials and
tribulations of which St Paul speaks are the sufferings
and tribulations of *an apostle*.[2] Peter did not receive the
whole world as his flock without hearing that love's
utmost was asked of him, without hearing the death he
was to die: 'Another shall gird thee and lead thee
whither thou wouldst not' (John 21: 15-19).

Authority and 'ministry'

Our inventory of New Testament texts would be incomplete without a brief look at its vocabulary. Some
expressions the New Testament uses frequently, others
it avoids or uses only rarely.

Among the latter are those expressing in Greek the
ideas of authority and power:[3]

[1]Thus, in St Matthew's Gospel, 16: 21-3 is followed by 16: 26-7;
the 'If any man will come after me' follows the confession of Peter
(Matt. 16: 24; Luke 9: 23); Matt. 17: 22-3 is followed by 18: 1-4
(cf. Mark 9: 30-6); Matt. 20: 17-19 followed by 20: 20-8; James and
John shall drink of the chalice, Matt. 20: 20 ff.; Mark 10: 35 ff.

[2]The apostle's sufferings: Col. 1: 24 (cf. J. Kremer, *Was an den
Leiden Christi noch mangelt. Eine interpretationsgeschichtl. u exegetische
Untersuchung zu Kol.* 1, 24b, Bonn, 1956); Acts 20: 19-27; Luke 8: 15
(cf. L. Cerfaux, 'Fructifier en supportant l'épreuve', in *Rev. bibl.* 64
[1957], pp. 481-91). Cf. R. Asting, *Die Verkundigung d. Wortes im
Urchristentum* . . . , Stuttgart, 1939, pp. 489-96 (the Servant of Isaias);
difficulties and death are the normal outcome of faithful witness,
pp. 589 ff., 599; St Paul, pp. 627, 635 ff.; in the Apoc., pp. 655 ff.—
Death, setting the seal on the apostolate for Paul: Phil. 2: 17-18;
cf. 2 Cor. 12: 15; Acts 9: 15-16; 20: 24; 21: 13. For the apostles to
whom the liturgy ascribes the title of martyr: John 17: 18-19; Hebrews 13: 7 (with Fr C. Spicq's commentary, p. 421).

[3]See the Concordances, the corresponding notices in the diction-
aries (especially *T.W.N.T.*) and, for the question as a whole, A.
Dumas, 'L'Ordre dans l'Eglise', in *Foi et Vie*, November-December

Taxis, order: ten instances in the New Testament, seven of them in Hebrew in connection with the orders of Aaron and Melchisedech.

Time, in the sense of a dignity or honour, is very rare: used only of Christ, the steward of the house of God (Hebrews 3: 3) and of the priesthood of Aaron and Christ (Hebrews 5: 4).

Arche occurs twelve times in the New Testament in the sense of 'power' ('hierarchy' is never used): three times it applies to magistrates, the civil power (Luke 20: 20; Titus 3: 1): the other nine times to the Powers that Christ has overcome or will overcome. In no case does the word refer to authorities within the Church.

Exousia, authority, power, is used ninety-three times in the New Testament.[1] Often it refers to the authority of God or Jesus Christ,[2] three times to the authority of earthly magistrates. Seven texts are relevant to our subject, i.e., to ecclesiology, the apostolate, the ministry. In five of them, Jesus gives authority to his disciples to cast out devils: Matt. 10: 1; Mark 3: 15; 6: 7; Luke 9: 1; 10: 19. In two, the term refers to the

---

1953, pp. 489-514; K. H. Schelke, *Jüngerschaft und Apostelamt. Eine biblische Auslegung des priesterlichen Dienstes,* Freiburg, 1957, pp. 36 ff. and 38, n. 1.

[1] In the Gospels, the word is almost always applied to Jesus, who 'teaches' with authority (5 times), 'pardons' with authority (4 times), 'acts' with authority (7 times), 'will judge' (twice). It is also used of God (3 times), the devil (5 times), earthly magistrates (9 times), the heavenly powers (13 times). In the Apocalypse, it is used 19 times (for God, the Lamb, the satanic beasts). In eleven cases the word has the weakened sense of permission, liberty (e.g. 1 Cor. 8,: 9). Cf. A. Dumas, *loc cit.,* p. 495.

[2] See A. Feuillet, 'L'Exousia du Fils de l'Homme (d'après Mc. 2: 10-28 et par.)', in *Rech. Sc. rel.,* 42 (1954), pp. 161-92.

authority vested in an apostle as minister of God's work in the Church: 2 Cor. 10: 8; 13: 10.

Epitage, authority to command, with the power to bind others: Titus 2: 15. When the command comes from God, St Paul clearly complies with it (Rom. 16: 26; 1 Cor. 7: 25; 1 Tim. 1: 1; Titus 1: 3); he possesses this authority and could exercise it (Titus 2: 15), but often he prefers not to use it (1 Cor. 7: 6; 2 Cor. 8: 8).

I have confined myself here to terms expressing the *idea* of authority. It is certain that authority is included, *as a reality*, in Christ's institution of the apostolate and in the apostles' institution of certain ministries, and similarly in the fact of mission, even when this is not inflated without qualification by the Jewish concept of *saliah*, envoy. We are not at the moment concerned with the reality of authority, which seems to me to be undeniable, but with the notion of it. That is why I have kept to the level of vocabulary.

The term which generally expresses this function in the New Testament is *diakonia*, which means 'service'; but its specific connotations are so rich and varied that it is best to translate it as 'ministry'.[1] In the case of particular ministries, all the words designating them refer to a *task* or *activity* as if to a definite service in the community. Frequently, they are borrowings from the vocabulary of everyday life, with no religious connotation; they become religious terms—and then how forc-

---

[1] See above, p. 36, n. 3. Cf. for example Luke 1: 2; Acts 6:4; 19:22; 20: 24; 21: 19; Romans 11: 13; 12: 7; 1 Cor. 3: 5; 12: 5; 2 Cor. 6: 3; Eph. 4: 11; I Peter 4: 11.—See also the art. *latreuo* (in *T.W.N.T.* vol. IV, pp. 58-64, H. Strathmann) and *leitourgeo*, *ibid.*, pp. 221 ff.; and, when it appears, the art. *uperetes*.

ible they are!—only when they are lived with Christ, in Christ, and for Christ. This is true even of the word *ordinari, ordinatio*. Here they are:

apostles, doctors, prophets: 1 Cor. 12: 28;

evangelists, teachers: Eph. 4: 11;

pastors: Eph. 4: 11; 1 Peter 5: 2f.; John 21: 15-17;

bishops, overseers: Acts 20: 28; Phil. 1: 1; 1 Tim. 3: 2; Titus 1:7;

priests, ancients, elders: Acts 11: 30; 14: 22; 15: 2; 20: 17; 21: 18; 1 Tim. 4: 14; 5: 17 and 19; James 5: 14; 1 Peter 5: 1;

diaconos, minister: frequent in a general sense of servant; as the title of a function, cf Phil. 1: 1; 1 Tim. 3: 8 f.;

leader, chief, official in charge: Acts 18: 22(?); Hebrews 13: 7 and 17a;

proistamenos, president: Rom. 12: 8; 1 Thess. 5: 12; 1 Tim. 5: 17 (presbyters);

steward, bailiff, manager: (Luke 12: 42); 1 Cor. 4: 1; Titus 1: 7.

Historical Development of Authority

The Church of the Martyrs and Monastic Catholicism

The Church of the Martyrs spans the period from the apostles to the peace of Constantine; and what I here call monastic Catholicism spans the period from then to roughly the middle of the eleventh century, with the proviso that the great historical epochs I am here distinguishing must not be considered as heteregeneous nor as strictly limited to a chronological period before and after which we find none of their features existing. I wondered at first whether it was not necessary, from our present standpoint, to distinguish as two separate periods the Church of the Martyrs and the Church from the fourth to the tenth century. In spite of certain slight reservations I shall indicate, I do not think this advisable. As regards the idea of authority, they both belong to the same ecclesiological world. Newman calls the five centuries from St Gregory to St Anselm the Benedictine period.

The notion of authority in the Church of the Martyrs combines into one the following three features or values which we shall deal with one after the other. They are :

40.

a strong insistence on authority; a very close link with the Christian community; a marked charismatic or spiritual character.

The insistence upon authority has never been greater than in the writings of St Ignatius of Antioch (in 109-110) and of St Cyprian (between 245 and 258). This insistence is all the stronger in that the religious or mystical value of salvation or of grace coincides completely with the juridical status of the authority presiding over a society and regulating its life. This fact is stated over and over again by Ignatius, Cyprian and also, be it noted, by Irenaeus (circa 180), and St Hippolytus (circa 200) who, like Origen soon after, calls the bishop 'Prince'.[1] We need only refer to a few of St Ignatius's formulae. They are so vigorous that critics formerly doubted their authenticity, in view of what they considered their outrageous 'Catholicism'. By being subject to their bishop, the Magnesians or the Trallians are subject to God himself or to Jesus Christ (Magn. III, 1-2; cf. VI, 1; Tral. II, 1). It is the Spirit who cries out in Ignatius : 'Cleave to your bishop, to the presbyterium and the deacons' (Phil. VII).

The link with the community—it might almost have been as well to put this characteristic first because, for early Christianity, the primary reality is the *ecclesia.* This word—and in this respect it differs from the word 'Church' as very often used today—means the Christian community, the assembly or the unity of Christians. St

[1]For Hippolytus, cf. Treatise on the Apostolic Tradition, 2 and 3 (and J. Lécuyer, 'Episcopat et Presbytérat dans les écrits d'Hippolyte de Rome', in *Rech. Sc. rel.*, 41 (1953) pp. 30-50). For Origen, cf. *In Matth. comment.*, 16: 8 (ed. Klostermann, p. 492 seq.); other references in J. Lécuyer, article, *Episcopat*, in *Dic. de Spiritualité*, vol. V. col. 887.

42 *Power and Poverty in the Church*

Cyprian says '*Plebs sacerdoti adunata et pastori suo grex adhaerens. Unde scire debes episcopum in Ecclesia esse et Ecclesia in episcopo.*'[1] It is this *Ecclesia* in her entirety which exercises her spiritual motherhood by her charity, unity, prayer and penance; she is the true and adequate reality whose actions are holy and sanctifying.[2]

This same interpretation of *Ecclesia* is found in the liturgical texts, which are the expression of tradition. The *Ecclesia* is the assembly of the brethren established by an act of the Lord and by his presence in their midst.[3] The ancient liturgy has no 'I' distinct from the 'we' of the whole community. The celebrant, that is, the president of the assembly and the head of the community, speaks in the name of all, for he is one with all its members. Several letters dating from the subapostolic period are written by the community and by its head, and the two are inseparably linked.[4] In these letters,

[1]66. 8 (Hartel, p. 733): 'The Church is the people united to its pontiff, and the flock abiding with its shepherd. This will make you see that the bishop is in the Church and the Church in the bishop'. At the time of writing, Cyprian was away from his community.

[2]See K. Delahaye, *Erneuerung der Seelsorgsformen aus der Sicht der Frühen Patristik* (*Untersuchg. z. Theol. d. Seelsorge*, 13), Freiburg, 1958. For a somewhat later period, see above all Augustine: P. Rinetti, 'Sant' Agostino e l'Ecclesia mater', in *Augustinus Magister*, Paris 1954, pp. 827-34; F. Hofmann, *Der Kirchenbegriff des hl. Augustinus*, Munich, 1933, pp. 268-75; J. Ratzinger, *Volk und Haus Gottes in Augustius Lehre von der Kirche*, Munich, 1954, pp. 142-3.

[3]Cf. J. A. Jungmann 'Wast ist Liturgie?' in *Zeitsch. f. kath. Theol.*, 1931, pp. 83-102 (reproduced in *Gewordene Liturgie*, Vienna, 1941, pp. 1-27); B. Luykx, 'Prière de l'Eglise et Participation active', in *Quest. Lit. et Par.*, Sept., 1959, pp. 271-88; see also *Dict. de Spiritualité*, article *Eglise*, vol. V, col. 379-80.

[4]For instance the letter of Clement of Rome to the Church of Corinth. Eusebius says of a letter of Denys of Corinth: 'it is addressed by him and by the Church he governed to Xystus and the Church of Rome' (*Hist. Eccl.*, VII, 9. 6).

there is a constant alternation of assertions of the hierarchical principle and assertions of the community
principle.[1] When in 1950-52, I was preparing my book
on the laity, I examined not only the texts but the facts
of the early history of the Church. I discovered everywhere in each generation and in the four spheres of
faith, worship, the apostolate and the Church's social
life, a union between the hierarchical structure and the
communal exercise of all Church activities. The laity took
an active part in the life of the Church as a whole. St
Cyprian puts into words a principle echoed on all sides
by tradition. He says: 'I have made it a rule, ever since
the beginning of my episcopate, to make no decision
merely on the strength of my own personal opinion
without consulting you (the priests and the deacons),
without the approbation of the people.'[2] In fact, the
whole Church community, the laity especially, took part
in the election of bishops and the choice of ministers.
They supplied information for councils and shared in the
institution of those customs by which the various communities to a great extent regulated their own lives.[3]

[1]Ignatius of Antioch, for instance, connects the hierarchical and
the community principles (*Magn, VI* and *VII; Smyrn., VIII*), but in-
sists on the hierarchical principle as the very condition of the community's existence (*Magn., III; XIII; Trall., II-III.* 1; *Philad., super-
scription and IV*). For Clement, see especially Cor. XLIV and LXIII
(hierarchical principle) and XXXIV. 7; XXXVII. 5 (community).
See also J. Colson, *L'Evêque dans les communautés primitives* (*Unam
Sanctam*, 21, Paris, 1951).

[2]Epist. 14: 4 ('*nihil sine consilio vestro et sine consensu plebis mea privatim
sententia gerere*'). Cf. Epist. 34: 4, 1 (*tractanda . . . non tantum cum collegis
meis, sed cum plebe ipsa universa*); Epist. 32.

[3]For all this see F. Cabrol 'Initiatives individuelles dans la liturgie
et Magistère de l'Eglise', in *Quest. Lit. et Par.*, June 1927, pp. 129-52,
and especially Y. M-J. Congar, O.P., *Lay People in the Church*, London,
1957, p. 230 seq.

Their intervention as occasion arose was accepted all the
more willingly since the early Church, whilst possessing
a firm canonical structure, wanted to be ready for any
movement inspired by the Holy Spirit. And God is
pleased to make his will known through the humblest
and the least esteemed of his children.

Nevertheless, the bishops were the men who posses- ✓
sed the principal *charismatic gifts* in the community.
The passage in St Paul: 'But the sensual man perceiveth
not these things that are of the Spirit of God: for it is
foolishness to him, and he cannot understand: because
it is spiritually examined. But the spiritual man judgeth
all things: and he himself is judged by no man' (1 Cor.
2: 14-15) had all true believers in mind. It was the statement of a principle of Christian anthropology and has
been understood as such by tradition. However, a special
application of the text was very soon made in regard to
the bishops, the heirs of the apostles or of their immediate successors and, like them, possessed of charismatic
gifts as well as pre-eminent in dignity and authority. In✓
the early Church, in fact, the mystical and the juridical
elements were closely interwoven and the idea of grades
of spirituality[1] was linked with that of grades of dignity.
The bishop was then looked upon as a head or a 'prince'
(cf. above, p. 41, n. 1) and, at the same time as a spiritual

[1]See A. M. Königer, 'Prima sedes a nemine iudicatur', in *Beiträge
z. Gesch. des christl. Altertums u. der byzantin. Literatur*, A. Ehrhard-
Festgabe, Bonn, 1922, pp. 273-300. For two expressions of this idea
of the bishop as a spiritual man: St Hippolyte, *Refutatio omnium
haeresium*, I. Proemium (there is a kind of 'tradition' of the Holy
Spirit and of Succession in the *Charis* of the Apostles); *De aleatoribus*,
c. 3: 'Episcopium, id est Spiritum Sanctum per impositionem manus
cordis excepimus hospitio'.

man endowed in a pre-eminent way with the gifts of the Spirit. It was as such that he was chosen, for it was his duty to lead God's people. His actions, and in a more general way, all the decisive factors in the life of the Church, whether due to decisions emanating from the authority of the bishop or of synods, or from some other source, were attributed to God's intervention. A text like the following from the acts of the council held at Carthage in the Spring of 252 is evidence of a fact it would be easy to verify in a great number of examples: 'It has pleased us, under the inspiration of the Holy Spirit and in accordance with admonitions given by the Lord in many manifest visions.'[1] The life of St Cyprian is marked by visions and supernatural admonitions. From this time forward, we find a continuous series of texts which use, in regard to all the decisive acts in the life of the

---

[1] In St Cyprian, *Epist. LVII*. 5 (Hartel, p. 655). For Cyprian, see A. Harnack, 'Cyprian als Enthusiast', in *Zeitsch. f. Ntl. Wiss.*, 3 (1902), pp. 177-91. For the early Church, H. Bacht. 'Die prophetische Inspiration in der kirchlichen Reflexion der vormontanistischen Zeit.' in *Theol. Quartalsch.*, (and *Scholastik*), 1944, pp. 1-18; G. Bardy, *La Théol. de l'Eglise de S. Clément de Rome à S. Irénée* (*Unam Sanctam*, 13) Paris 1945, p. 129 seq., 144, 150; *La Théol. de l'Egl. de S. Irénée au Concile de Nicée* (*Unam Sanctam*, 14), 1947, p. 53 seq., 56, 176, 190, 195 note 1. Warnings and signs had already been followed among the pagans when appointments to office were made (see J. Béranger, *Recherches sur l'aspect idéologique du Principat*, Basel, 1953, p. 164 seq.). A similar practice is sometimes found in the Middle Ages (V. Fuchs, *Der Ordinationstitel von seiner Entstehung bis auf Innozenz III*. Bonn, 1930, p. 56 seq.). St Bernard pays heed to them when deciding between Innocent II and Anacletus II, and Gratian lends his weight to the idea, *C.* 16, *C VIII*, qu. 1 (Friedberg, 595=Origen, *Hom.* 22 *ad c.*27 *Numer.*, *n.* 4, *P.G.* 12, 238). It is God who controls the life of the Church.

Church, the words *inspirare, inspiratio, revelare, revelatio,* and others of similar type.[1]

In the early Church authority was that of men who were like princes in a community which was wholly sanctified, *plebs sancta,* and overshadowed by the Spirit of God. The Church leaders were all the more conscious of their authority in that they saw it as the vehicle of the mystery of that salvation which God wishes to accomplish in his Church. They wanted to be, and knew that they were, moved by the Spirit, but they also knew that the Spirit inhabits the Christian community and in the exercise of their authority they remained closely linked to this community.

From Constantine to Gregory VII

It might be assumed *a priori* that this concept would be more or less perverted or abandoned by the episcopate during the period following the peace of Constantine. The clergy were given important privileges, the bishops became *illustri,* and for all practical purposes, ranked with the senators.[2] They were invested with public authority within the framework of the Empire, even in the sphere of the secular life of the cities. The bishop was the defender of the people, especially of the poor and the weak. He shared in the administration of

[1]See for bibliography and documents in my *La Tradition et les traditions, Essai historique,* Paris, 1960, Excursus B, 'Permanence de la "Revelatio" et de l' "Inspiratio" dans l'Eglise', pp. 151-66.

[2]For what follows cf. S. Mochi Onory, *Vescovi e Città* (sec. IV-VI), Bolonga, 1933; J. Gaudemet, *L'Eglise dans l'Empire romain (IVᵉ-Vᵉ siècles), (Hist. du Droit et des Instituitions de l'Egl. en Occident, III)*, Paris, 1958.

justice, he exercised a measure of control over the magistrates and the city assemblies. He co-operated in defence preparations (the maintenance of the town walls, for instance) and in actual defensive operations. The bishops frequently called on the imperial authority for support. We have only to remember, to take one example, the history of Donatism. Further, Church laws often became laws of the Empire, which undertook to see that they were respected. Under these conditions, we ought perhaps to expect that authority would change its character and that it would acquire a much more secular, much more juridical meaning, based simply on the relation of superior to subordinate. It would cease to open onto the higher sphere of a marked charismatic action on God's part and on to the lowest sphere of the influence of the action of the community, and so close in on itself and become authority for its own sake, authority pure and simple.

Such a danger was very real. It was comparable and in a line with the danger of a hellenization or rationalization of doctrine resulting from an effort to produce a symbiosis of doctrine and pagan philosophical culture. The two cases are parallel and were more or less contemporary.

Monasticism has often been represented as a protest against a Church that had become too worldly, too rich, too powerful in a physical sense for an eschatological Christianity which taught that the world should be opposed. In monasticism it was possible for a charismatic or spiritual authority to continue to exist, an authority which should be exercised when the aim is to form the spiritual man, to introduce the soul to 'the philosophy of Christ'. In fact, this is the type of

authority found among the patriarchs of monasticism or
the legislators of the religious life, the authority of those
who are purely and simply 'men of God'. And, in the
last analysis, this authority is that of the Spirit himself
shining through the purity of the *vir Dei*.[1] This type of
authority did in fact acquire a kind of autonomy in the
Church in relation to the ordinary hierarchical structure. This was the case in the East.[2] Both Origen and
the pseudo-Areopagite held views which tended to link
the illuminating and sanctifying effect of hierarchical
acts with the interior and spiritual holiness of the
minister. From the beginning of the eighth century and
as a result of the monothelite quarrel and still more the
iconoclast crisis during which the monks had been the
champions of orthodoxy, there was a real transfer of
spiritual direction and of the exercise of the power of
the keys from the hierarchical priesthood to the monks,
even when the latter were not priests, because it was
clear that they were the genuinely spiritual men and
friends of God. As is well known, this oriental tradition

[1]See O. Casel, 'Benedikt von Nursia als Pneumatiker', in *Heilig
Ueberlieferung (Festgabe I. Herwegen)*, Münster, 1938, pp. 96-123.

[2]For what follows see J. Stiglmayr, 'Die Lehre von den Sakra-
menten u. der Kirche nach d. Ps.-Dionysius', in *Zeitsch. f. kath.
Theol*, 22 (1898), pp. 246-303; K. Rahner, 'La doctrine d'Origène
sur la pénitence', in *Rech. Sc. rel.*, 37 (1950), pp. 47-97, 252-86, 422-56
(tends to 'ecclesiasticize' Origen); K. Holl, *Enthusiasmus und Bussge-
walt*, Leipzig, 1898; H. Koch, 'Zur Gesch. d. Bussdisziplin u. Bussge-
walt in d. oriental. Kirche', in *Hist. Jahrb.*, 21 (1900), pp. 58-78; J.
Hörmann, *Untersuchungen zur griechischen Laienbeicht*, Donauwörth,
1913; M. Viller, *Exemplar ideale monasticum et sacerdotale in Oriente
Graeco usque ad saec. nonum*, in *Commentarii pro Religiosis*, 8 (1927),
p. 206 seq.; I. Hausherr, *Direction spirituelle en Orient autrefois (Orient,
Christ, Anal.*, 144), Rome, 1955, p. 105 seq.; J. T. McNeill, *A
History of the Cure of Souls*, London, 1952, p. 307 seq.; Y. M-J.
Congar, 'Conscience ecclésiologique en Orient et en Occident du
VIe au XIe siècle', in *Istina*, 1959, pp. 187-236 (p. 223 seq.).

was revived or continued in the institution of the *Startsi* or elders of Holy Russia. These monks who were rarely priests exercised a wholly spiritual authority as men of God[1] in a ministry of spiritual direction and confession.

Was there not a similar phenomenon in the West, not only in particular cases where a purely spiritual influence was brought to bear, apart from all hierarchical authority (and this happens at every period), but in the particular organization of Celtic Christianity down to the twelfth century? There was no diocesan pattern, that is, there were no specific territories under the authority of bishops, but a whole complex of spheres of spiritual influence. A 'saint' had his own sphere of influence in which he was in a sense the permanent spiritual lord of a given place. A territory was affiliated to a holy man, and eventually there was a grouping with a monastery at its centre, and the jurisdiction belonged to the Abbot who was often, but not necessarily, in bishop's orders. Sometimes even, as at Kildare, jurisdiction was in the hands of an abbess. Authority was attributed to the man of God, and not to a particular grade in the priestly hierarchy.[2]

[1]Cf. K. Holl, op cit., p. 154; I. Smolitsch, *Leben u. Lehre der Starzen*, Vienna, 1936.

[2]A. Bellesheim, *Geschichte d. kathol. Kirche in Irland*, 3 vol., 1890-1900, vol I, p. 322 seq.; L. Gougaud, *Les Chrétientés celtiques*, Paris, 1911; 'La question des abbayes-évêchés bretonnes' in *Rev. Mabillon*, 11 (1922), pp. 90-104; J. Chevalier, *Essai sur la formation de la Nationalité et les Réveils religieux au Pays de Galles des origines à la fin du VI s.*, Lyons and Paris, 1913, p. 361 seq., 374 seq.; V. Fuchs, op. cit., pp. 195-211; J. Ryan, *Irish Monasticism, Origins and Development*, Dublin, 1931; W. Delius, *Geschichte d. Irischen Kirche von ihren Anfängen bis zum 12 Jahrh.*, Munich, 1954; Bede, *Hist. Eccl.*, III. 4, has a characteristic passage on Iona.

Yet it would be a mistake to see any *opposition* between this type of authority and that exercised by the bishops during the period from the peace of Constantine to the Gregorian reform. In the first place, it is a fact that many of these bishops were monks or at least men trained in a monastic setting and who ordered their lives on a similar pattern, often with a nostalgic longing for the religious life. To name only a few of these, there are St Basil, St John Chrysostom, St Augustine, St Martin, St Germanus of Auxerre, St Patrick, Eucherius of Lyons, Faustus of Riez, Lupus of Troyes, Caesarius of Arles, Martin and Fructuosus of Braga, Isidore of Seville, and finally the most representative of them all, St Gregory the Great.[1] From St Augustine's time until the twelfth century, all the archbishops of Canterbury were monks.

The bishop, whether or not a monk, is a spiritual man, a man of God. The oldest sections in the Latin ritual of ordination state his duties rather than his powers. The bishop must devote himself to an assiduous study of Holy Scripture,[2] to prayer, fasting, hospitality. He must welcome, listen to and help everybody, he must practise almsgiving. He is to edify his people by word of mouth

---

[1]Cf. P. Rémy Oliger, *Les évêques réguliers. Recherches sur leur condition juridique depuis les origines jusqu'à la fin du moyen âge*, Paris-Louvain, 1958, p. 15 seq.; for the monastic ideal of the bishop, see St Athanasius, *Epist. ad Dracontium*, n. 7 seq. (*P.G.*, 26, 532).

[2]St Ambrose in 374; '*Intentionem et diligentiam circa scripturas opto assequi*' (*De off.*, 1. 3: *P.L.*, 16. 24)); St Augustine, Epist. 21 (*P.L.*, 33. 88): St Gregory *Reg. Past.*, II, 11 and G. Hocquard, 'L'idéal du pasteur des âmes selon S. Grégoire le Grand', in *La Tradition sacerdotale. Etudes sur le sacerdoce*, Le Puy, 1959, pp. 143-67 (p. 155). St Gregory often refers to the study of scriptures as one of the necessary qualifications for one to be elected bishop (cf. *Registr.*, XI, 37; XIII, 14; XIV, 11; ed. M.G.H., *Epp.*, vol. 2, p. 309, 12, p. 382, 3, p. 340, 4).

and by the celebration of the liturgy, and in so doing, he is to be aware not of his *dominium* or *potestas*, but of his *ministerium*, to use the words the Catholic West owes to St Augustine.[1] God is the primal and sovereign agent of this edification. The phrases 'God has revealed, God has inspired' constantly recur as during the preceding period. Thus a *spiritual* as well as a pastoral authority was exercised in the hierarchical authority. This was in accordance with the ideal of *prodesse* as contained in *praeesse*, that had been universally accepted since St Augustine.[2] Men felt that this was true, even if they were not (yet) Christians. When the praetorian prefect Probus sent his subordinate Ambrose, then only a catechumen, to take up at Milan the post of *Consularis* of Liguria and Emilia, he told him: *'Vade, age, non ut judex, sed ut episcopus.'*[3] A bishop therefore represented a whole ideal of care for men's welfare, of justice, disinterestedness, welcome, in short an essentially moral ideal of authority.

This ideal we find attained by St Ambrose,[4] St

---

[1] This is already found in Optatus, V. 7. For Augustine, cf. D. Zahringer, *Das kirchliche Priestertum nach d. hl. Augustinus*, Paderborn, 1932, p. 125 seq.; F. Hofmann, op. cit., pp. 257-60.

[2] See 'Le hiérarchie comme service', in *L'Evêque dans l'Eglise universelle* (Unam Sanctam, Paris, 1961).

[3] Paulinus, *Vita Ambrosii*, c. 3, sect. 8.

[4] Ambrose himself said he did not wish to be a conqueror but a physician: *De fide*, 1. 11 (*P.L.*, 16. 579). We know the famous passage of Augustine on Ambrose: *'Suscepit me paterne ille homo Dei et peregrinationem meam satis episcopaliter dilexit. Et eum amare coepi primo quidem non tamquam doctorem veri, quod in Ecclesia tua prorsus desperabam, sed tamquam hominem benignum in me . . .'* (*Conf.* V. 13, 23—*P.L.*, 32. 717). For *episcopaliter* we may refer to the distinction made by St Jerome (*In Tit.*, c. 1, v. 8—*P.L.*, 26, 603) between the hospitality of a layman who entertains a *few* persons, and that of a churchman, a bishop, who has a welcome for *all*.

Augustine,[1] and finally by St Gregory the Great.[2] The
author of the *Regula Pastoralis*, so widely read in the
Middle Ages, was in fact himself a living model of the
spiritual exercise of authority. Not only did he achieve
his ideal of living a life in which personal sanctification
and the exercise of the ministry were combined, but he
also succeeded in exercising the supreme authority *in a
Christian manner*. This means, in the first place, that
authority is exercised in a genuine spirit of service and
so with a sincere sense of humility. For St Gregory the
formulae *Servus servorum Dei*[3] and *cunctorum sacer-
dotum servus sum*[4] were not mere official phrases. Over
and above the exercise of authority and in the very act
of exercising it, he took a genuine interest in the welfare
of the men under his command.[5] He loved and respected
their progress in virtue as resulting from their own free
will. He took care to explain to them the reasons for any
of his own decisions in the light of some good or some
truth which their souls instinctively sought.[6] In a word,

[1]See F. Van der Meer, *Saint Augustin pasteur d'âmes*, French translation, Paris-Mulhouse, 2 vol., 1955; M. Jourjon 'L'évêque et le
peuple de Dieu selon S. Augustin', in *Saint Augustin parmi nous*, Le
Puy-Paris, 1954, pp. 149-97; 'L'évêque comme membre du peuple de
Dieu selon S. Augustin', in *Bull. des Facultés cathol. de Lyon*, N.S., 11
(1952), pp. 21-41.

[2]In addition to G. Hocquard, cited above, p. 50, n. 2, cf. Fr
Heiler, *Altkirchliche Autonomie und Päptslicher Zentralismus*, Munich,
1941, pp. 224-8.

[3]See the heading of letters written by St Gregory when he was
pope.

[4]Reg. V. 37; M.G.H., Epp., I, p. 323—*P.L.*, 77. 747 B.

[5]*Summus igitur locus bene regitur, cum is qui praeest, vitiis potius quam
fratribus dominatur*' in *Reg. Past.* II. 6 (*P.L.*, 77. 36 C).

[6]In a letter written in February 601 to Theoctista, the Emperor's
sister, Gregory notes that the apostle Peter himself explained to the
Church the reasons for his baptism of Cornelius: '*Quaerelae fidelium*

he exercised his authority like a kind of supreme and universal Father Abbot, combining the tender care of a mother with the authority of a father.[1] The Church for him was not a vast organization or a system but a community of men moving towards the perfection of charity.

Not all the popes have followed this course. Yet, we should note at this point that if Rome succeeded in obtaining, over and above her power, the *authority* of her primacy, it was in large part due to the value and the wisdom of her answers to all the questions which were put to her from every region of Christendom. Genuine authority is moral authority.

Hence the great bishops of the centuries we have understandably called those of monastic Catholicism were very careful to relate authority to its transcendent spiritual principle. They also preserved its relationship to the Christian community which was still what they understood by the word *ecclesia*. At this period in fact the primal and decisive reality in ecclesiology was still the *ecclesia* itself, that is, the totality, the community, the unity of the faithful. This may appear to be a truism, but ten years of study of and reflection on the history of the ecclesiological doctrines have convinced me that it is not. It is a statement whose importance is primordial. The whole concept of authority in the treatise *De Ecclesia* and the whole balance of the treatise itself depends upon it. For the Fathers and the Early Christ-

non ex potestate, sed ex ratione, respondit, causam per ordinem exposuit' (Reg. XI, 27; M.G.H. Epp., II, p. 293). This is the exact opposite of a remark made by an important member of the Curia: 'Authority's proper characteristic is that it has not to give any reasons'.

[1]*'Curandum quippe est, ut rectorem subditis et matrem pietas et patrem exhibeat disciplina'*, Reg. Past., II. 6 (*P.L.*, 77. 38 A).

ians, the *ecclesia* comes first. Then, in the *ecclesia,* come
the *praepositi ecclesiae,* the presidents or heads of the
Christian community.[1]

The head of the Church, the bishop, is in the first place
himself a Christian, and he says so. St Augustine constantly tells his flock: 'I am a bishop for your sake, I am
a Christian together with you', 'a sinner together with
you', 'a disciple and a hearer of the Gospel together with
you', *vobis sum episcopus, vobiscum christianus.*[2]

The foundation of all this and of patristic ecclesiology,
which continued to be that of the early Middle Ages, is
doubtless the fact that the Church is composed of men
and that all that is done within the Church is aimed
formally and immediately at the formation of spiritual
men. Ecclesiology and anthropology are not in separate
compartments and the former is a continuation of soteri-
ology which is itself but one chapter in Christology.
This is why all the images and types in Scripture, in
which is expessed any aspect of the spiritual destiny of
men in relation to the Covenant God offers them, are
continually and easily applied to the *ecclesia.* What is

[1]This is the vocabulary used by St Cyprian and St Augustine.
Later, the term was to be *praelati ecclesiae* (St Thomas). The important
thing is not to reserve the name 'Church' for the body of men who
are the leaders *of the Church,* who govern *in the Church.*

[2]For this formula see *Sermo* 340. 1 (*P.L.,* 38, 1483); cf. *Enarr. in Ps.*
126. 3 (37. 1669); *De gestis cum Emer.,* 7 (43. 702); *Serm. ined.* 17.
8 (46. 880); *Serm. Denys.* 17. 8 (*Miscell. Agost.,* I, p. 88)—'*Christiani
propter nos, praepositi propter vos*'; *Sermo* 46. 2 (38. 371); 91. 5 (569)
cf. *Contra Crescon. II,* 11, 13-14 (431 474).—The Christians are all
servi or *discipuli,* Augustine their bishop is *conservus, condiscipulus:*
Sermo 340. 1 (38. 1483); *Enarr. in Ps.* 126. 3 (37. 1669); cf. *Sermo*
179. 7 (38. 970); 23. 2 (38. 155); 292. 1 (38. 1320); *Guelferb.* 324
(*Miscell. Agost.,* I. p. 566).—'I am a sinner together with you and like
you, I beat my breast': *Sermo* 56. 11; 135. 7 (38. 382 and 749). Cf.
M. Jourjon, mentioned above.

involved is not a system or a juridical set-up but a body of men praying, fasting, doing penance, asking for grace, engaging in a spiritual combat and struggling for the triumph in themselves of the spirit of Jesus Christ. This is why authority is *moral* and requires men who are themselves spiritually alive. On the other hand, it is obvious that if the Church is considered to be a supra-personal possessor of rights, a juridical personality enjoying a divine authority conceived as juridical, then these themes from spiritual anthropology no longer apply.

Under such conditions it is also true that authority is still exercised in conjunction with the community. The celebrated formulae: *Qui praefuturus est omnibus, ab omnibus eligatur,*[1] and *Nullus invitis detur episcopus,*[2] date from the councils and popes of the fourth and fifth centuries.

One form taken by this effort to win the agreement of the community was the care shown, at least in the fourth and fifth centuries, in reporting to this community or in keeping it informed of facts which today would be carefully withheld from its appraisal or even from its

[1] This is St Leo's formula in *Epist.* 10. 4 (*P.L.*, 54. 628); cf. 10. 6 (634); 13. 3 (665), etc. This may be compared with the following passage which comes at the beginning of the rite of the consecration of a bishop in the Gallican rite and dates from about the year 800: '*Ut igitur praefuturus omnibus electus ex omnibus universis sacris sacrandisque fiat, omnium precibus adjuvemur, omnium pro ipso oratio incumbat, cui exorandi pro omnibus pondus imponitur*' (L. Duchesne, *Origines du culte chrétien,* p. 380 seq.).

[2] This is the formula of Celestine I in *Epist.* 4, *c.* 5 (*P.L.*, 50. 434). It occurs again in the Councils of Orleans (549) and Paris (557), and in Gratian's *Decretum,* C. 13 D., LXI (Friedberg, 231). There are similar formulae as early as 314—the Council of Ancyra, canon 18 (Bruns I. 69). See my *Lay People in the Church* and J. Gaudemet, op. cit., p. 332.

knowledge. We have only to read in this connection the
sermons in which Augustine gave his people an account
of his line of conduct and of the principles on which he
wished to base the co-operation of his clergy in his work
as their bishop.[1] He did not hesitate to go so far as to
give a frank statement in public on a delicate business
involving one of his priests who had come to an arrange-
ment in which his own private interests had been too
cleverly promoted. Who would do anything of the sort
today? By giving all his flock an account of the way in
which he wanted his priests and clerics to live with him,
Augustine lifted the whole life of the *ecclesia* onto so
lucid a plane that he ensured for himself the enlightened
and full consent of the faithful.

On the other hand, in the context of the Christian
Empire, clerics and bishops obtained important immuni-
ties in regard to the secular jurisdiction.[2] Later, within
the Church herself, canon law was to weave a kind of
Noe's cloak around the prestige and honour of clerics,
bishops and Roman dignitaries.[3]

These privileges are part of the body of legal measures
which henceforward contributed their share towards
making the clergy a class apart. Among these measures,
celibacy was one of the most important,[4] but others,
such as the introduction of a special costume from the

---

[1]*Serm.* 335. 3 seq., and 356. 2 seq. (*P.L.*, 39. 1570 seq. and 1575 seq.).
For St Augustine, the acknowledgement of one's own weaknesses
was demanded if one were to be able to admonish other people. Cf.
Contra Epist. Parmen., *III.* 5, 26 (*P.L.*, 43. 103).

[2]Cf. J. Gaudemet, op. cit., p. 240 seq. (bibliography).

[3]*Constitutum Sylvestri*, c. 3 (a document forged during the pontificate
of Pope Symmacus, 498-514) in C. Mirbt, *Quellen z. Gesch. d. Papsttums*, No. 193.

[4]Cf. Hinschius, *Kirchenrecht*, vol. I, p.144 seq. ; J. Gaudemet, op.
cit., p. 156.

end of the early part of the fifth century,[1] effectually initiated a considerable change in the relations between the faithful and the presidents of the community, priests or bishops. In fact, the difference between the two categories tended to be not only a difference of function as it had been since the beginning within the framework of service in the *ecclesia*, but a difference in Christian living. Clerics were to observe a special rule of life modelled more or less on that of the monks and inspired by the levitical regulations of the Old Testament. Thus, whilst in the Church of the Martyrs there was a tension, not inside the Church between the various categories of Christians, but between the *ecclesia* and the world, henceforth within a society entirely Christian, tension grew inside the Church or within Christian society, between monks or priests on the one hand and laymen on the other. I am well aware that this statement is too simplified and categorical; it needs to be qualified and clarified, and this cannot be done here. It was necessary however, even at the risk of over-simplification, to draw attention to this point which is extremely important for our subject.

[1]In 428, Pope Celestine I upbraided Honoratus abbot of Lerins, who had been appointed bishop of Arles, for introducing a special dress, namely, the tunic and belt. This was the monastic habit and an innovation. Hitherto, priests' dress was exactly the same as that of other men. Even in the celebration of the liturgy they merely wore *clean* clothes. Celestine wrote to the bishops of the Narbonne province: 'We should be distinguished from others, not by our dress but by our knowledge, by our conversation, not by our manner of life' (*Epist.* 4. 1, 2—*P.L.* 50. 431). See L. Christiani 'Essai sur les origines du costume ecclesiastique', in *Miscellanea Guil. de Jerphanion* (*Or. Christ. Per.*, XIII, 1947), pp. 69-80; H. Norris, *Church Vestments, their Origin and Development*, London, 1949; Cletus della Iacono, *De habitu ecclesiastico, Diss. historico-critica*, Rome, 1953.

The main lines of the facts we have just summarized remained characteristic of Christianity during the early Middle Ages as it existed in the West among the nations emerging from the barbarian invasion and converted to Catholicism. But there were certain differences which I must be allowed to do no more than enumerate here without producing documentary evidence to substantiate their existence : 1. The word *Ecclesia* at this period indicated Christian society and included the Empire or the various kingdoms as well as the Church properly so called; 2. This *Ecclesia* was governed by two authorities, or in the terms used since Gelasius, by two 'pre-eminent persons', the royal and the priestly; 3. The authority of the priesthood was essentially understood as the authority of the power of the keys, that is, of a sacred power that was both sacramental and judicial, and gave or refused entry into heaven.

Hence an historical study aiming to cover all the ground would have to consider the concept and exercise of priestly authority in every sphere of social life and over the princes themselves as princes. This is obviously beyond the scope of the present paper.

Priestly Authority in the Middle Ages

We are convinced that the reform begun by St Leo IX (1049-54) and continued with such vigour by St Gregory VII (1073-81) represents a decisive turning-point from the point of view of ecclesiological doctrines in general and of the notion of authority in particular.

We know that this reform not only aimed, like all reforms, to purify the Church—it was accompanied by powerful spiritual movements in favour of the 'apostolic life' such as the canons regular and even the eremitic life—but also to deliver the Church from the power of laymen. It aimed to rid itself of its identification with political society, an identification indicated by the word *Ecclesia* itself which meant both the mystical Body and the Empire with no distinction made between them. In short, it meant Christian society. To bring this about, Gregory VII claimed for the Church the completely autonomous and sovereign system of rights proper to a spiritual society.

The foundation of the ecclesiastical edifice was the pope whose authority emanated directly from a positive divine institution. Gregory VII claimed the sovereign rights of this authority not only over the Church but also over kings and their kingdoms. To support his claims, he had asked churchmen Peter Damian to begin with) to discover the maximum number of juridical texts in favour of this view. In point of fact, a whole series of canonical collections owes its existence to this request. For all these reasons, the eleventh century reform set in motion a powerful wave of canonical studies. Schools were founded, among them that of Bologna, in which, from this time onwards, both the Roman and the canon law were studied together. Research brought to light a great number of texts; efforts were made to classify, harmonize and systematize these. The science of canon law had well and truly begun.[1]

From the point of view in which we are now inter-

[1] Cf. P. Fournier, 'Un tournant de l'histoire du droit', 1060-1140, in *Rev. hist. Droit frs et étr.*, 41 (1917), pp. 129-180; W. Ullmann, '*The Growth of Papal Government in the Middle Ages*', London, 1955, ch. XI, p. 359 seq.; Y. M-J. Congar, 'Der Platz des Papsttums in der Kirchen-frömmigkeit der Reformer des xi. Jahrh', in *Festgabe Hugo Rahner*.

ested, there emerged such a considerable development
of an authority methodically asserting and claiming its
rights, that it is possible to speak of a new chapter in the
history of the notion of authority itself, although it is
quite true that the situation was not entirely new and
that popes or bishops had already asserted and claimed
such rights. This development was so powerful because
it was not purely juridical or purely academic. On the
contrary, it was due to powerful personalities and a vast
and profound 'mystique'. St Gregory VII in the first
place, then St Anselm of Canterbury and later St Thomas
Becket, who became immensely popular after his death,
these are the men who initiated or brought forward these
assertions or this claim to these rights. Not that they
claimed them for themselves personally (they were
wholly disinterested), but for their authority, and on the
basis of a very theological and very supernatural 'mystique'. What interested them all was absolute *Justice*
that is, a theonomy (a divine law) which was expressed
in a system of Church law, and even more precisely in
the rights of the Pontiff.[1] The same attitude is found in
Innocent III, not perhaps in Innocent IV who was more
strictly a jurist, but certainly in Boniface VIII in his own
somewhat questionable and equivocal way. The strength
of a movement always lies in its 'mystique'. In the

[1]For Gregory VII, see H. X. Arquillière, *St Gregory VII*, Paris, 1931;
A. Nitschke, 'Die Wirksamkeit Gottes in der Welt Gregors VII', in
Studi Gregoriani, vol. V, Rome, St Paul, 1956, pp. 115-219; our study
mentioned on p. 59, n. 1. For St Anselm cf. Y. M-J. Congar, 'L'Eglise
chez S. Anselm', in *Spicilegium Beccense*, I, Le Bec and Paris, 1959, pp.
371-99 and several papers in the same collection. For St Thomas
Becket, cf. M. Pacaut, *Alexander III*, Paris, 1956, p. 396 seq.; on his
popularity, R. Foreville, *Le Jubilé de S. Thomas Becket du XIIIᵉ au XVᵉ* s.
(1220-1470), Paris, 1958.

movement we are now considering, what was characteristic was the fact that its 'mystique' was formulated in
and, one might almost say, invested with legal principles,
and a genuine political theology.

This was not achieved without submitting certain
themes and certain texts to a legalistic interpretation.
I myself attach very great importance to one fact which
I have personally studied in a few given cases, namely
the translation into terms of law (and of rights!) together
with a specific application to the pope and to the pope
alone, of themes and texts that originally and up to this
period belonged to the realm of spiritual anthropology.
I have studied this change of level and meaning in the
case of Jer. 1: 10; 'Lo, I have set thee this day over the
nations, and over kingdoms, to root up, and to pull down,
and to waste, and to destroy, and to build, and to plant',[1]
in the case of 1 Cor. 2: 15 and 6: 3; 'But the spiritual
man judgeth all things: and he himself is judged by no
man. Know you not that we shall judge angels? how
much more things of this world?'; less directly and less
fully in the case of 1 Pet. 2: 9, 'you are a kingly priesthood', and in a few other instances. Jer. 1: 10 becomes
an assertion of the supreme authority of the pope and
of his right to depose kings. One of the last occasions in
which this text was used in this sense was in Pius V's
bull *Regnans in excelsis* deposing Queen Elizabeth I.
(Elizabeth II harboured no resentment; she visited Pius
V's successor, John XXIII, on the very day allotted in the
calendar to the feast of the former.) 1 Cor. 15 becomes
a new formulation of the old principle *Prima Sedes a*

[1] See *'Ecce constitui te super gentes et regna'* (Jer. 1: 10) in 'Geschichte
und Gegenwart' in *Theologie in Geschichte und Gegenwart, Festg. M.
Schmaus*, Munich, 1957, pp. 671-96.

nemine judicatur and 1 Cor. 6: 3, *'angelos judicabimus, quanto magis saecularia'* becomes an assertion of the right of priests, but more especially and supremely of the right of the pope, to judge secular powers.

We have also studied a fact which seems to have escaped Mgr M. Maccarone, who has written the history of the expression *Vicarius Christi* as a papal title. The use of the title has continued but its meaning has changed. Its older sense in Catholic *theology* was that of a visible representation of a transcendent or heavenly power *which was actually active* in its earthly representative. The context and atmosphere surrounding this idea were those of the actuality of the action of God, Christ and the saints working in their representative. This is a very sacramental, iconological concept, linked to the idea of constant 'presences' of God and the celestial powers in our earthly sphere. It is this quality of actuality and of a 'vertical' descent and a presence which has its source in the celebrated text in Luke 10: 16, *'Qui vos audit, me audit; qui vos spernit, me spernit'*. Although this quality does not disappear, it is overlaid by another quality which also is not entirely new—what is new is its marked predominance over the former one—namely, the idea of a 'power' given at the beginning by someone, by Christ, to his 'vicar', that is, to a representative who takes his place and who hands on to those who come after him, in an historical sequence of transmission and succession, the power thus received. The predominant feature is not a vertical movement, an actual presence, an iconological representation, but the 'horizontal' transmission of a power vested in the earthly jurisdiction and which, although received from on high, is yet genuinely possessed by this jurisdiction which uses it in the same way as any authority may use the power attached to it.

The modern 'mystique' of authority in the Church is derived from the movement whose characteristics we just described. But—and this is where its strength lies, once again, strength comes from the 'mystique' and not from the legal aspect—it has combined the actuality of the power possessed with the vision of the 'vertical' descent of divine power upon the actual historic authority. One is actually obeying God when one obeys his representative. Unless I am mistaken, this is, in particular, the view of St Ignatius Loyola as it is explained for instance by Fr Hugo Rahner.[1] Fr Rahner moreover does not find any difficulty in linking St Ignatius Loyola with the first Ignatius of Antioch, with St Irenaeus and St Augustine (who inspired Gregory VII: cf. Bernheim's studies and those undertaken under his direction), etc.[2] This shows that although there was an innovation, it was still in continuity with a tradition. I believe however that the spirit of the time introduced something new into this continuity, namely, a certain legalistic aspect.

We see this legalism at work in the importance attached to the formal validity of authority, to its possession of a title in law. There is no insistence on the need of an actual intervention of God's grace, nor therefore on the need for man to pray for this intervention and to prepare for it by bodily mortification, by explicitly relating the exercise of authority to sacred acts such as

[1] *Servir dans l'Eglise, Ignace de Loyola et la Genèse des Exercices*, Paris, 1959 (*Ignatius v. L. und das geschichtliche Werden seiner Frömmigkeit*, Graz).

[2] The mystical idea of an actual or sacramental presence was linked with the juridical idea in the case of papal authority by means of the theme of the Pope as *St Peter himself*. This is the case as early as St Leo, *Serm.* 3 *de Natali*, 4 (*P.L.*, 54. 147) etc.

the celebration of the mysteries, fasting, chastity, prayer, etc.[1] In short, legalism is characteristic of an ecclesiology unrelated to spiritual anthropology, and for which the word *ecclesia* indicates not so much the body of the faithful as the system, the apparatus, the impersonal depositary of the system of rights whose representatives are the clergy or, as it is now called, the hierarchy, and ultimately the pope and the Roman Curia.

It is a fact that 'Church' is sometimes understood by the theorists of ecclesiastical power or papal authority as indicating clerics, priests and the pope.[2] This use of the word was completely unknown to the Fathers and the liturgy. It is a fact that in a large number of modern documents, the word 'Church' indicates the priestly government or even quite simply this government's Roman courts. It is distinct from the faithful, from men in general and outside and above them. Here is one example from hundreds which could be given: 'The Church is given the task of feeding the flock of Jesus Christ.'[3] But the Church is herself this flock. This change of meaning is serious. In the first place, it is out of keeping with scriptural, patristic and liturgical usage. Further, it runs the risk of separating the 'Church' from the sphere in which men are trained in the spiritual life. I would like to point out in this respect a problem which,

[1]This process can already be seen at work in the Pseudo-Isidore (cf. G. Hartmann, *Der Primat des römischen Bischofs bei Pseudo-Isidor*, Stuttgart, 1930, pp. 86-7 and 89-96, for some significant comparisons with early Christianity in the strict sense of the term).

[2]See examples in *Lay People in the Church*, p. 42, n. 22

[3]Mauro Capellari, in the opening address of his *Triomphe du St-Siège et de l'Eglise* (trad. fr., vol. 1, p. 18). In patristic terminology the phrase would have been '*rectores dominici gregis*', see Gelasius I, Epist. 6. 2 (ed. Thiel, *Rom. Pont. Epist.*, p. 326).

as far as I know, has never been considered, namely the application of the directives of the Gospel, not only to individuals but to the Church as such. Is it the individual alone who must be the servant and not the master, who must forgive offences, bless his enemies and not curse them? Have themes such as these any longer a place in an ecclesiology identified in practice with a treatise on public ecclesiastical law?

Further, under these conditions, instead of being seen as a relationship of superior to subordinate *within* the vast system of mutual love and service between Christians who are Christians as the result of a grace for which each is accountable to all, does not authority run the risk of being posited *first and foremost* as *authority for its own sake*, and so of being looked upon in a purely juridical and sociological way, and not from a spiritual and Christian standpoint?

It is obvious that Christians and men of God anxious to work for his kingdom and devoid of all self-interest, have shaped their lives in accordance with this juridical concept. At a more prosaic level, this is true of conscientious churchmen. But it has favoured the growth of the idea of the priest as *governing* his parish, as exercising a *regimen,* as *regens.*[1] It has favoured the growth of the idea of the bishop and the pope as *judges,*[2] of the pope as a *sovereign,* since he is the vicar of Christ,

---

[1]We have found many examples in a paper on 'Aspects ecclésiologiques de la querelle entre Mendiants et Séculiers dans la sec. moitié du XIII⁰ s. et le début du XIV⁰⁰' in *Arch. Hist. doctr. litt. du M. Age,* (1961). Cf. T. M. Parker, 'Feudal Episcopacy', in *The Apostolic Ministry,* ed. by K. E. Kirk, London, 1946, pp. 351-86 (p. 381).

[2]Parker, ibid., p. 383. Cf. A. L. Mayer Pfannholz, mentioned below, p. 66, n. 2, *(Ged. Casel).*

Rex regum et Dominus domimantium.[1] It has favoured
the growth of the idea of the Church as *queen* of mankind, since she is the Bride of Christ who is the ruler
of the world.[2] It cannot be denied that, from the eleventh
century onwards, authority and in particular the
supreme authority of the pope, borrowed many of the
features of the vocabulary, insignia, ceremonial, style
and ideology of the imperial court. These factors sometimes go back to pagan days and even, by way of the
hellenistic monarchy of Alexander, to the Persian
paganism of the fourth century B.C.[3] Even the title of

[1]These words from Apoc. 19. 16 are often used in this sense (cf.
J. Hashagen, *Staat u. Kirche vor der Reformation*, Essen, 1931, pp. 503-5)
especially by Innocent III (cf. my short article in *Catholicisme*). On
the papacy as the world's supreme tribunal, cf. A. Mayer Pfannholz
'Gregor VII. u. Heinrich IV. im Lichte der Geistesgeschichte' in
Zeitsch f. deutsche Geistesgesch., 2 (1936), p. 153 seq.; 'Der Wandel de
Kirchenbildes in der Geschichte', in *Theol. u. Glaube*, 32 (1940), pp.
22-34.

[2]Cf. Mayer Pfannholz mentioned in the previous note (*Th. u. Gl.*,
p. 27) and also by the same author, 'Das Bild der Mater Ecclesia im
Wandel der Geschichte', in *Pastor Bonus*, 53 (1942), pp. 33-47; 'Das
Kirchenbild d. späten Mittelalters u. seine Beziehungen z. Liturgie-
geschichte', in *Vom christl. Mysterium. Ges. Arbeiten z. Gedächtnis v.
O. Casel*, Dusseldorf, 1951, pp. 274-302 (p. 284 seq.). The idea of the
Church as queen is frequent in iconography but is not so common in
theological writings or official documents. Yet it is evident in the
gradual change from the notion of Mother Church to that of the
Church as *magistra* and *domina* which is extremely common. For
Gregory VII, cf. the paper quoted above (p. 59, n. 1), notes 17
and 23-5.

[3]In my view the most relevant study is that of P. E. Schramm,
'Sacerdotium und Regnum im Austausch ihrer Vorrechte, Eine
Skizze der Entwicklung z. Beleuchtung des "Dictatus Papae"', in
Studi Gregoriani, vol. II, pp. 403-57. On imitation of the Byzantine
court, cf. also R. Elze, 'Das "Sacrum Palatium Lateranense" im 10 u.
11. Jahrh', in *Studi Gregoriani*, vol. IV pp. 27-54; W. Ullmann op.
cit., p. 310 seq. On the transfer of the ceremonial of the Hellenistic
monarchy to the Roman and Byzantine emperors and the Persian

Curia assumed by the papal administration was borrowed from the secular vocabulary and, at the time,
there were those who did not fail to point this
out.[1]

Protests were made. We shall not cease to insist that
one of these has never been taken seriously enough,
either at the time or since, by the historiographers. I
refer to the protest represented by the more or less anti-
ecclesiastical spiritual movements so frequent in the
twelfth century and which continued in the Franciscan
spiritual movement down to the fourteenth century
when it was succeeded by Lollardism and subsequently
by the Hussite movement. All these movements, each
from its own point of view and within its own terms of
reference said the same thing: 'Less pomp and more of
the Gospel! You are Constantine's Church, not the
Church of the apostles.' St Bernard, who did battle with
Arnold of Brescia, Henri de Lausanne and the neo-
Manicheans, did not scruple to repeat these explosive
criticisms. He wrote to Eugenius III: 'You allow your-
self to be over-burdened with decisions you have to give
in all kinds of external and secular cases. As far as you
are concerned, I hear of nothing but awards and "laws".

sources of this ceremonial, see L. Bréhier, 'L'Origine des titres im-
périaux à Byzance' in *Byzant. Zeistch.*, 15 (1905), pp. 162-77; J. B.
Bury, *The Constitution of the Later Roman Empire*, Cambridge, 1910;
A. Alföldi *Die Ausgestaltung d. monarchischen Zeremonielles am römischen
Kaiserhof* (*Mitteilg. d. deutschen Archeolog. Inst. Röm. Abt.*, 49), 1934;
J. Maurice, 'Les Pharaons romains', in *Byzantion*, 12 (1937), pp. 71-
103. For the part played by an imperial ideal in canonical ideology, J.
B. Sägmüller, 'Die Idee von der Kirche als Imperium Romanum im
kanonischen Recht', in *Theol. Quartalsch*, 80 (1898), pp. 50-80.

[1]The word appears in the latter part of the eleventh century; cf.
'L'Ecclésiologie de S. Bernard', in *Saint Bernard théologien* (*Anal. S.
Ord. Cist.*, 9, 1953), pp. 136-90 (p. 184).

All this, as well as claims to prestige and riches, goes back to Constantine not to Peter.'[1]

In a more general and perhaps more profound way, theology preserved many elements of the ancient ecclesiology in a balanced view which lasted until the death of the two greatest thirteenth century doctors, Thomas and Bonaventure. In St Thomas, for instance, the idea of the Church as *congregatio fidelium* is very much alive, and includes the theology of the return to God of man made in his image. Authority is not looked upon as a mere formal and juridical value; it is linked to the spiritual gifts, to the achievement of Christian perfection which is the perfection of charity, and so, by the same token, to the achievement of spiritual liberty and the gift of self in loving service. Matt. 16: 19 is interpreted as referring principally to Peter's confession of faith. The theology of the new law, as formulated in the I^a–II^{ae} qu. 106 and in the scriptural commentaries, is completely evangelical and certainly represents a fundamental category in St Thomas's ecclesiology.[2]

We should be guilty of a serious omission if we failed to mention also what we might call the right of conscience. This principle was a vital force down to the Reformation, after which the condemnation of its abuse involved the end of its use. This is a vast field of research demanding special study. It includes, to begin with, the right of resistence to tyranny in the political sphere, and the right to enter religion or to change from one Order

[1]See the article mentioned in the preceding note, pp. 164-5, 183.

[2]See 'The Idea of the Church in St. Thomas Aquinas', in *The Mystery of the Church*, London, 1960, pp. 97-117; 'L'apostolocité de l'Eglise selon S. Thomas d'A.', in *Rev. Sc. ph. th.*, 44 (1960) pp. 209-24. I shall be publishing at some time in the future a study of the *congregatio fidelium*.

to another. It then deals with the protection of the poor
and the weak—a traditional function of episcopal authority—and the notions of unjust excommunication, the
right of protest, the right also to disobey *filialiter et
obedienter* to quote from a letter of Robert Grosseteste
to the pope.[1]

Harnack remarked that it was at the time when the
formulation of the nature of ecclesiastical power had
reached its point of perfection that this power began to
be questioned, denied and attacked. It is a fact that the
authority of prelates of every degree was never insisted
on so much as in the fourteenth and fifteenth centuries.
The thunderclap of 31 October 1517 was only the first
of a violent storm. On the Continent the Reformation
refused the right of any human authority whatsoever to
enter into the field of man's religious relationship with
God. This relationship was to be conditioned by the
authority of God alone, and this authority was simply
and solely that of his word as contained in scripture.

From the Council of Trent until the present day

The Reformation questioned authority not only in its
historical forms, but as a principle. And the Reformation
was roughly contemporary with the rise of the great
forces that created the modern world (the sciences of
observation, the primacy of individual personality, the
passion for invention and continual progress, historical

[1]*'Filialiter et obedienter non obedio, contradico et rebello'*—*Epist.* 128
(ed. H. R. Luard, Rolls Series, 1861, pp. 636-7), and cf. Br. Tierney,
'Grosseteste, and the Theory of Papal Sovereignty', in *Journal of
Ecclesiast. History*, 6 (1956), pp. 1-17.

and philosophical criticism, perhaps even the beginnings of rationalism).

The Church's reaction became clear from the time of the Council of Trent onwards. It consisted in the two-fold process which the Church normally brings into operation when she is seriously challenged. On the one hand, she reasserted her authority and gave it a greater degree of centralization. On the other hand, she revised the idea and the practice of authority on the moral and pastoral planes.

She reasserted her authority and not only her own, but the authority of God, of his revelation (Council of the Vatican), of Christ (Christ the King), of the state (encyclicals of Leo XIII), and the authority of parents. Ecclesiology, as far as the instruction of clerics and of the faithful is concerned, became fixed in a set pattern in which the question of authority is so predominant that the whole treatise is more like a hierarchiology or a treatise on public law.[1] In this assertion of authority, the papacy receives the lion's share. The idea of authority, the exercise of authority in contemporary Catholicism, are first and foremost the idea and the exercise of papal authority. The pope is really *episcopus universalis*. Each individual Catholic has a much more immediate relationship with him than with his own bishop, as far as the general pattern of his Christian life is concerned. The encyclicals tell him what he ought to think, the liturgy is regulated by Roman documents, as are also fasting, canonical preparation for marriage, the *ratio studiorum*

[1] See *Rev. Sc. ph. théol.*, 1947, p. 77 seq.; *Lay People in the Church*, ch. II; 'L'ecclésiologie, de la Révol. fr., au concile du Vatican, sous le signe de l'affirmation de l'autorité', in *L'Ecclésiologie au XIXᵉ siècle* (*Unam Sanctam*, 34) Paris, 1960, pp. 77-114.

of seminaries and the canonically erected faculties. The
saints we venerate are those canonized by Rome; religious congregations ask Rome for the authorization of
their rule and it is from Rome that the secular Institutes
have received theirs. Rome intervenes directly in the
question of adapting apostolic methods to the needs of
the times (worker priests, *Mission de France*). She keeps
a sharp eye on publications, books, reviews, even cate-
chisms, and, on occasion, orders their suppression. In
short, the exercise of authority in the modern Catholic
Church is largely that of its central and supreme seat
in Rome.

At a time when the modern world is attempting to
build its life on the principle of the individual personality, even to the point of disregarding or denying the
objective rights of God and of his law, the Catholic
Church since the sixteenth century has put into practice
a genuine 'mystique' of authority in which the influence
of the Society of Jesus has doubtless played its part. This
'mystique' may be characterized as the notion of a
complete identification of God's will with the institu-
tional form of authority. In the latter, it is God himself
whose voice we hear and heed.[1] The fairly wide margin
which the Middle Ages still left for the subordinate's
appraisal is, for all practical purposes, reduced almost to
nothing. The pope is the visible Christ, 'gentle Christ on
earth' as St Catherine had already said. And every
superior is to some extent the visible Christ. Some have
even spoken of a real presence of Christ under the

[1]There is a very typical article by Fr P. Charles, 'Vicarius Christi',
in *Nouv. Rev. théol.*, 1929, pp. 443-59 (reproduced in *L'Eglise, sacrament du Monde*, Paris, 1960, pp. 111-17). See also, by the same author,
'Le pouvoir absolu dans l'Eglise', in *Nouv. Rev. th.*, 1925, pp. 129-36.

pontifical species.[1] Further, the present period has seen, in France at least, a frequent and new use of the terms *hierarchy* and *magisterium*,[2] which, at the level of terminology, indicate a healthy but very powerful insistence on authority.

A certain absolutist sense given to authority and to obedience[3] presupposes a whole development in ecclesiological ideas. To give an account of this growth would involve nothing less than a complete history of the ideas in question. I must be content to stress one point which seems to me to be of more than marginal importance. The image of the Bride, as applied to the Church, was drawn at a very early date towards the image of the Body by the Pauline theme of the *una caro* (Eph. 5).[4] From both the biblical and the theological aspects, these images are complementary yet distinct. 'Body' indicates identity, 'Bride' indicates otherness, a face to face encounter, the Church related to Christ as

[1]Mgr. Durand: cf. *Semaine relig. d'Oran*, 25 Oct. 1930, n. 493. For a proper assessment of such comparisons, cf. Ch. Journet, *L'Eglise du Verbe incarné*, vol. I, p. 496 seq., 519, 606.

[2]The ancient meaning of the word *magisterium* is 'teaching, doctrine'. In the Middle Ages, the word commonly indicates the situation or the activity of a master or, in a more general sense, authority to decide or to govern. Applied to the Church, the word sometimes has a meaning somewhat akin to the one it has today, for instance in Bernard de Fontcaude, *Contra Vallenses*, ch. 2, n. 4 (*P.L.*, 204. 799 B, 1185+). However, *Magisterium* in the sense of 'the teaching Church' seems to be a modern usage.

[3]Obedience becomes the fundamental virtue. Cf. the bull *Exsurge* which condemned Luther: *Nervum ecclesiasticae disciplinae, obedientiam scilicet, quae fons est et origo omnium virtutum* (Mansi, vol. XXXII, col. 1053).

[4]Cf. Claude Chavasse, '*The Bride of Christ, An Enquiry into the Nuptial Element in Early Christianity*', London, 1939.

to her Lord, her head in the sense of Lord.[1] To the extent that the theme of the Church as Bride has been absorbed into that of the Church as the Body of Christ, the authority of God has been seen as wholly, one might almost say physically and automatically present, in the authority of the Church; the absolute standard of the divine authority has become, so it would seem, identified with and invested in the human standard of the ecclesiastical authorities. It is true that during the eleventh and twelfth century struggles between the priesthood and the secular powers, arguments were based on the rights of the Church as the Bride of Christ and so the Mother of Christians, and these rights were those of God himself.[2] It is obvious that this development would scarcely have been possible if there had been no progress beyond the ancient meaning of *Ecclesia* as indicating the Christian community.

If the medieval clergy who did not have to go out in search of their flock, and who enjoyed considerable privileges, were scarcely called upon to show zeal, the clergy of today are. The Council of Trent by the impetus it provided and the measures it took, began the creation

[1]See Bossuet, *IVme Lettre à une Demoiselle de Metz*, and C. Dumont, *Les voies de l'unité chrétienne* (*Unam Sanctam*, 26), Paris, 1954, p. 134 seq., 223 seq., Engl. trans., *Approaches to Christian Unity*, London and Baltimore, 1960.

[2]See our article on St Anselm, mentioned above p. 60. There are innumerable texts. Here are two examples: John of Salisbury writing under the name of Theobald, archbishop of Canterbury, to King Henry in 1160 (Epist. 127) said: '*Si vultis, immo quia vultis Christian habere propitium, Sponsam ejus (quae est Ecclesia, cujus et ipse caput est, illa enim Capitis Corpus) studeatis habere propitiam*' ('*Letters of John of Salisbury*', I, ed. W. J. Misser and H. E. Butler, London, 1955, p. 220). Gregory IX, *Ep. Si nobilis vir* (29 May 1228): Christ and the Church are Bride and Bridegroom and so are one body. The Church cannot be despised or molested without despising Christ.

of a new clergy.[1] Previously, priesthood often existed
apart from personal holiness of life, in spite of the fact
that Councils and episcopal regulations never ceased to
insist on the need for priests to be holy men. After the
Council of Trent, especially in France during the seven-
teenth century, priests were given rules of conduct
similar to those of the religious life: mortification,
prayer, avoidance of every kind of worldliness, etc. At
the same time, the clergy emerged from the uncultured
state so often characteristic of its members in the Middle
Ages. A link was reforged, somewhat like that existing
in the patristic period, between the office or the authority
and the personal religious quality of the priest's life.

Yet there is one important difference between the
nineteenth century or even the first years of the
twentieth, and the fourth or fifth centuries; the priesthood is much less monastic, if not from the ascetical
point of view, at least from that of the life of contempla-
tion, of the assiduous study of scripture, of preaching
based on the bible and the mysteries of the faith. The
bishops have always been absorbed by the cares of
administration, or by matters in dispute. This is true of
the bishops in the fourth, fifth and sixth centuries and
still more of those of the twelfth to the fifteenth,[2] and
these were involved in more secular business.[3] In our

[1]Typical examples are Bl John of Avila (cf. A. Duval, *Quelques
idées du Bl J. d'A sur le ministère pastoral et la formation du clergé: Suppl. de
la Vie spirit.*, August 1948, pp. 121-53), and St Charles Borromeo.
See H. Jedin and P. Broutin, *L'Evêque dans la tradition pastorale du
XVIIᵉ siècle*, Bruges, Paris, 1953; P. Broutin, *La réforme pastorale en
France au XVIIᵉ siècle*, 2 vol. Paris-Tournai, 1956.

[2]T. M. Parker, mentioned on p. 65, n. 1.

[3]See the article quoted above, p. 67, n. 1: Fourth Council of the
Lateran (1215), can. 10.

own times they are absorbed by administrative and financial worries. Fr Combalot humorously observed in the middle of the nineteenth century: 'Instead of *"Accipe baculum pastorale"*, it would be more to the point to say *"Accipe calamum administrativum ut possis scribere, scribere, scribere usque in sempiternum et ultra!"* '.[1] As for priests, they are ceaselessly taken up with pastoral 'cases', with a ministry of personal help and support, with repair and rescue work. But all of them, bishops and priests, have a very keen sense of their pastoral and apostolic responsibility. The adjective 'apostolic' represents in itself a whole programme, it signifies a historical change in the application of the term 'apostolic' which in modern times has come to mean zealous and having the missionary spirit.[2] It cannot be denied that the exercise of authority in the Church today is marked by a predominance of pastoral care over prelacy, of tasks and responsibilities over the claiming of privileges. And yet an ecclesiology that is still too juridical, too remote from spiritual anthropology, continues to give a somewhat external character to the aims of authority, a character that is sometimes inclined to be sociological rather than interior and spiritual. 'The Church is anxious to do a great deal of governing, but she gives very little education'.[3] However, a post-Constantinian situation is increasingly making it imperative that, in a world where institutions are no longer enough for the believers' needs, priests should concentrate on training and encouraging

[1] Quoted by R. Aubert, *Le Pontificat de Pie IX*, Paris, 1952, p. 452.

[2] See L. M. Dewailly, 'Notes sur l'hist. de l'adjectif Apostolique', in *Mél. de Sc. rel.*, 1948, pp. 141-52; H. Holstein 'L'Evolution du mot "apostolique" au cours de l'histoire de l'Eglise', in *L'Apostolat (Problèmes de la Vie Religieuse d'aujourd'hui)* Paris, 1957, pp. 41-61.

[3] Complaint of A. Loisy, *Mémoires*, vol. II, p. 368.

men who possess strong personal convictions. Hence the mid-twentieth century is characterized by the re-discovery of men who are truly Christian *in their humanity itself*. There can be no doubt that authority will have increasingly to recover the spiritual character of the Church of the Martyrs and the Fathers and to take as its aim the building up of communities of Christian men.

In the nineteenth century, romantic literature, and often history also, had spread the idea that power and the holding of very high office offered an opportunity for greater enjoyment, for complete freedom to do as one liked and for helping oneself. The popes of the nine-teenth and the twentieth centuries and with them, the whole body of the bishops, have stood before the eyes of the whole world as men for whom power is respon-sibility and authority service.

Conclusion

If the history we have outlined had to be summarized in a few significant phrases and a few representative figures, we should doubtless say : for the Church of the Martyrs, the key words are *the Lord* and the *diaconia*; its typical hero is St Paul. For the Church of the Fathers and the monk-bishops, the words are *Ecclesia, Prae-positi Ecclesiae, Deus inspiravit, ministerium*; the typical heroes, Ignatius of Antioch and Cyprian, Ambrose, Chrysostom, Augustine, Gregory the Great. For the medieval period, the words are *Vicarius Christi, caput, Sponsa-Mater-Magistra, regere, potestas*, and the typical heroes, St Gregory VII, St Thomas Becket. For the modern or post-Tridentine period, the words are 'the Church' when its leaders are really meant, or 'the Hierarchy', 'the Magisterium', but also 'the laity' and 'apostolic'; and the typical heroes are St Ignatius Loyola, St Charles Borromeo, the *'Pius-Päpste'*, that is, Pius IX to Pius XII, Cardinal Suhard.

An overall view of this development reveals its fairly obvious direction, namely, towards a development of ecclesiology itself. One's first examination of any phenomenon is always all-embracing. It may be less exact than subsequent analyses but it includes far more. The community, the *ecclesia*, was first examined, then increasing attention was paid to the *potestas* of its head.[1] The first thing to be seen was the community *composed of Christian men*; then its structural pattern, its organization was examined. Everything was initially attributed to the transcendent cause, then the part played by ecclesiastics as 'means' became more clear, and not only so, but the consideration of their function absorbed attention almost to the exclusion of everything else, it being understood once and for all that God is the origin of all. The status of ecclesiastical authority is examined in detail. The history of the exegesis of Matt. 16: 18-19 is very instructive in this respect. Formerly, *'hanc petram'* was taken to mean the 'stone' of the confession of faith, and insistence was laid on Christ as the foundation. Later the text was held to refer to Peter alone. Similarly, Mary the Virgin was first seen as the Mother of Christ who is God, later her own privileges were studied in detail. In ecclesiology, God was above all

[1]The letter of Clement to the Corinthians is a letter from the Roman community. Pius IX promulgated the constitutions of the Vatican under the heading: *Pius, sacro approbante concilio.*

considered initially as directly at work; subsequently
attention turned to the created institution which possesses vicariously the powers given by God and of which
it is the depositary.

At the present time, we live in the period of rediscovery in breadth and depth of our own heritage. And
this is due above all to the active investigation of the
permanent sources: scripture, tradition, the Fathers, the
liturgy. This return to the sources has already begun to
emphasize the necessity of a certain rediscovery of the
two religious realities by reference to which authority
must find out the truth about itself. They are the living
God active among us through his grace, and the holy
community and brotherhood of the faithful. It is by
setting authority in an authentic relationship with these
two Christian realities that we shall be able to go
beyond legalism which consists in seeing the formal
validity of phenomena without penetrating to their
meaning. The movement back to the sources must go
forward until it restores a completely evangelical concept of authority, a concept that will be both fully
supernatural and fully communal. We are on the right
road, we have gone far to recover the *agape* beyond
mere moralism, the function of the laity, the community,
and our mission and service, as dimensions essential to
and co-extensive with Christian life. We have a better
understanding of the religious implications of the
covenant, and these involve our acceptance of God's
gift through faith, and the life of this gift of God within
us through the *agape*, the *diaconia,* witness and thanks-
giving. And this is all of a piece and stands or falls as
such. Since we are returning to a pre-Constantinian
situation in a pagan world, since we are aware that we

are in a minority and that it is our task to preach Jesus Christ, we are doubtless approaching a period in which, while we shall lose nothing of value acquired in the course of history, we shall recover wholly evangelical ways of exercising authority in the new world in which God calls us to serve him.

3

The Christian Concept of Authority

The pronouncements of Jesus and the apostles on the subject, and the passages from New Testament literature that I have quoted (cf. above, pp. 21-34), lead us to reflect on the actual concept of authority in the New Testament. It would not be enough simply to conclude that authority must be exercised in a spirit of personal unselfishness and service, though of course this would lead to genuine and profitable developments. It is true that the good shepherd gives his life for his sheep, does not feed himself but seeks the good of his flock.[1] It is true that he must not be demanding or grasping, but must make every effort not to be a burden to any in his care.[2] It is true that the faithful are our masters, since we are their servants: their welfare must decide how our effort shall be applied.[3] To know all this not by the

[1] Cf. Ezech. 34; Jer. 23: 1-6; John 10; Schelkle, *op. cit.*, pp. 39 ff.

[2] See Num. 16: 15; 1 Sam. 12: 3; Neh. 5: 14 ff.; 1 Thess. 2: 9; 2 Thess. 3: 8; Phil. 4: 15.

[3] It is told in the life of St Bonaventure how, on the way to the Chapter General at Assisi, he was stopped by a simple friar who asked his help and consolation. The Minister General gave him his full attention. To those who remonstrated with him, saying that he had better things to do, he replied: 'I am a minister, a servant: he is

intellect alone but in heart and conscience has been and never ceases to be the principle of true evangelical holiness for those who have offices of command in the Church and in the world. The measure of all things, in Christianity, is indeed the spirit of the beatitudes. This is an admitted fact: authority, in the Church, is 'not domination, does not impose itself by force; it is service, humility, unselfishness, self-sacrifice'.[1]

The Church itinerant

But Jesus was not content simply to remind men of the spirit in which authority must be exercised, or to transfer authority from the scribes and rabbis to the apostles, from the priesthood of Aaron to the ministers of the Gospel. He radically transformed the whole character and even the nature of authority.[2] And in the same way he was not content simply to replace the sacrifice of Moses and the priesthood of Aaron by another sacrifice and another priesthood, still of the same nature: he transposed them to another plane of reality. This is more than an analogy with the case of men. Sacrifice and priesthood, and also law, 'sabbath', covenant and temple, are bound up together so closely that one cannot change without the other changing, and the same 'newness' affects them all when the Son of God

my master . . . ' St Vincent de Paul often talked of 'the poor, our masters . . . ' When one is truly a servant, the other is the master and gives the orders; one does one's best to satisfy him.

[1] P. Broutin, *Mysterium Ecclesiae*, Paris, 1945, p. 255.

[2] W. Foerster notes that Luke 22: 25 is not concerned with the abuse or unworthy use of power, but with power itself, and every use of it (*T.W.N.T.* vol. III, p. 1097).

became flesh and the Holy Spirit was given (see Hebrews, and 2 Cor. 3).

The newness lies in this: we have passed from signs, announcements or preparations to realities. Or rather, we have taken a decisive step towards this passing over to reality. For *pure* reality is eschatological: it corresponds with the state in which all dominion and power shall be brought into subjection, when the externals that afflict us shall be things of the past, when perfect interiority shall be established, rooted in the final condition, 'God all in all'.[1]

Midway between the synagogue and the kingdom whose embryo she is in this world, the Church is the place where sacrifice, priesthood, law, sabbath and covenant are made new, as befits the time (*eon*) of Christ's coming and the gift of the Spirit. From then on they are in the hearts of men. Sacrifice and priesthood are spiritual, which does not mean metaphorical but corresponding to God's working *in man*.[2] The temple, the place of the presence of God, is the community of the faithful, a spiritual house of living stones, wherein are offered spiritual sacrifices acceptable to God through Jesus Christ (1 Peter 2: 5; cf. 1 Cor. 3: 10-17; Eph. 2: 19-22; 4: 11-16, etc.). There are still *things* in the Church exterior to man and God, because she is not yet pure reality: there are still sacraments, churches built of stone, ceremonies, powers, a coercive form of law, etc. But all that is secondary and subordinate to the essential,

[1]See my *Vaste Monde, ma paroisse*, Paris, 1959, pp. 56 ff. English translation, *The Wide World my Parish*, London and Baltimore, 1961.

[2]I may perhaps refer to my works: *Vraie et fausse réforme dans l'Eglise* (*Unam Sanctam*, 20), Paris, 1950; *The Mystery of the Temple* (trans. R. F. Trevett), London, 1962; *Sacerdoce et laïcat ...* (*Cogitatio fidei*, 4), Paris 1962.

which is men and the grace of the Holy Spirit within them.[1] The decisive value of what exists in the Church lies not in *things* as things but in living men who, through Christ and in view of his plenitude, build up the Body of Christ or the Temple of God, by faith and charity. Everything is relative to the living body of Christ, which is made up of the faithful. 'You are the body of Christ and individually members of it.'[2] That is the fundamental fact underlying our whole theme. In New Testament and patristic texts, the Church is never separated from the Christian life of Christian men, as a *thing* would be; the very word *Ecclesia* approximates very closely in meaning to what we now call the Christian community.

God all in all

There is one single source for the building up of this Christian community, Jesus Christ, the head from which the body has its whole life and increase,[3] the foundation-stone on which—it can almost be said, in which—the whole temple is built.[4] But from Christ onwards all that each receives is directed to the building up of his body. So each becomes a means of life and growth for all the rest.

[1]This is simply a summary of St Thomas' entirely evangelical doctrine on the nature of the 'new law' (which is the Gospel): *S.T.*, Ia IIae, q. 106, a.1 and 2; q. 107, a.1, ad 3; q. 108, a.1; *Com. in Hebr.*, c.8, lect. 2; *De Ver.*, q. 17, a. 5.

[2]See 1 Cor. 12: 5; Rom. 12: 5; 1 Cor. 6: 15; 12: 12 ff.; Eph. 1: 23; 4: 16; 5: 30; Col. 1: 24.

[3]Eph. 4: 15ff.; Col 2: 18 ff.

[4]Eph. 2: 19-22; 1 Peter 2: 4 ff.

Due allowance made, the same holds good of the physical universe because this too, in its own way, forms a whole.[1] And, with certain necessary transpositions, it is true of the spiritual sphere of destinies that are personal and yet entirely of Christ. That is why St Paul gives this general rule, of prime importance for us all: 'As every man hath received grace, minister the same one to another; as good stewards of the manifold grace of God.'[2] And that too is why St Paul repeats that, in the Body of Christ, each is the servant of all.[3]

In this statute of the life of the Body we can see an anticipation, a sign, a far-off hint of 'God all in all'. In fact, no Christian attitude can be considered in only two terms. Many pronouncements of Christian attitudes or, if one prefers it, of Christian ethics, are paralleled by very similar pronouncements from such schools of philosophy as Stoicism. But closer inspection reveals a very important difference: pronouncements on Christian ethics or Christian attitudes are not located only on the plane of a human perfection to be striven after; they always flow from their source, as it were, or proceed from their foundation—the attitude, and in

[1]P. de Saint-Seine, 'La biosphère', in *Etudes*, November 1948, pp. 166 ff., has some suggestive passages (he returns to the theme in *La découverte de la vie*, Paris, 1948): one species lives by another, and the balance of the whole is ensured by its parts; 'it is an immense web, a coat without seam'.

[2]1 Peter 4: 10; Cf. Gal. 6: 1-2; Rom. 15: 14; 2 Cor. 1: 4; Col. 3: 16; 1 Thess. 5: 11 and 14; 2 Thess. 3: 15; Hebr. 3: 13; 10: 24-5. Hugh of Saint Victor: 'Unusquisque non sibi soli habet, etiam id quod solus habet' (*De sacrum*, 1. II, p. 2, c. 2; *P.L.*, 176, 416); cf. St Peter Damian, Opusc. '*Dominus vobiscum*', c. 5-18 (*P.L.* 145, 235-46).

[3]Gal. 5: 13; cf. 6: 2; 1 Cor. 9: 19-23 ('all things to all men'); 2 Cor. 4: 5.

the end the nature, of God, revealed to us in human terms in Jesus Christ. Of everything a Christian receives, everything by which he lives and for which he is accountable to his fellows, God is the only source. And because this is so, because he himself does give to all, we too owe to all what we receive from him.

'Now, there are diversities of graces, but the same Spirit. And there are diversities of ministries, but the same Lord. And there are diversities of operations, but the same God, who worketh all in all. And the manifestation of the Spirit is given to every man unto profit ... But all these things, one and the same Spirit worketh, dividing to every one according as he will' (1 Cor. 12: 4-7 and 11; cf. for sense, Eph. 4: 4-16).

After St Paul, hear what Bernanos, a Christian says:

'Life teaches me that no man is consoled in this world who has not first given consolation, that we receive nothing that we have not first given. Between us there is only exchange. God alone gives, only God.'[1]

Jesus Christ the only Lord

We are now in a better position to understand the Christian idea of hierarchical office as service. It comes within the compass of the great truths we have just recalled: there is only one Lord; he distributes his gifts to individuals for the service of all and the building up of the Body-Temple: so each one of us, as the disciple

[1] G. Bernanos, *Les Enfants humiliés*, Paris, 1949, p. 36.

of Jesus Christ, becomes the debtor or servant of all.
Hierarchical offices organize this service.[1] Fr L. Laberthonnière has very rightly said (though he was mistaken
in thinking that he was in contradiction with St Thomas,
when he was in fact doing little but repeat him): 'The
exercise of authority in general is only one of the forms
of what we each have to do through others and for
others to further our common destiny.'[2] St Paul expressly
says that ordained ministers organize the ministry of the
saints, that is of Christians (Eph. 4: 12). They organize
it, but they also invigorate and animate it and drive it
forward. They are the drivers and the governors of the
Body in that condition of responsibility and universal
service which is the Christian condition itself.

To this end, there are temporary orders which relate
to individuals, the gifts they have received, the inner
call they have answered, the circumstances in which
life and Providence have placed them. We sometimes
speak of charisms in this sense; and this is allowable, if
we are careful to remember that 'charism' means simply
'spiritual gifts', and that established ministries by no
means stand outside the charismatic order. There are
also permanent orders, which organize the Christian

[1] Cf. K. H. Schelkle, *op. cit.*, p. 39, note: 'Dass alles Amt nur
Ordnung des Dienstes ist'—'Every ministry is only an ordering of
service'.

[2] 'Théorie de l'éducation', in *Essais de Philosophie religieuse*, pp.
261-2: the passage continues: 'Those who command and those who
obey have the same goal, and should be inspired by the same spirit.
The only difference is that those who command have a greater responsibility; they are specially answerable for the others in the
degree to which the others have been specially entrusted to them.'
Cf. below, p. 90, n. 1. For St Thomas, see *S.T.*, IIa IIae, q. 104, a.
1 and 4.

ministry in the sense of *diakonia* (see above, p. 25 f), that is, the whole Church seen as service, exercising the ministry, which might equally well be called the service, of the word or of worship.[1] Though it is often impossible to fix the frontier between the two domains, the subject of charisms, more particularly in teaching, is sometimes a regular ministry, sometimes the faithful independently of any previous nomination or ordination.[2]

The subsequent life of the Church developed along lines dictated by a separation, perhaps too clear-cut, between the two orders—which could be described as *ex spiritu* (by virtue of spiritual gifts) and *ex officio* (by virtue of an office), gifts of the individual and gifts of function. To keep them apart, and above all to regard the order of function as something alien to the order of personal spiritual gifts, would be a betrayal of the new Testament. And of theological tradition too: St Gregory links the vocation of ministers

[1]Ministry of the word: Luke 1: 2; Acts 6: 4; 19: 22; Rom 12: 7; 2 Cor. 5: 18 ff ; 2 Tim. 4: 5. Cf. the priestly service of the Gospel, Rom. 15: 16. The ministry of the Gospel becomes the ministry of justice, of the spirit, 2 Cor. 3: 7-9. For worship, the usual verbs are *latreuein* (Rom. 12: 1; cf 2 Tim. 1: 3; Phil. 3: 3 and, eschatologically Apoc. 7: 15; 22: 3)—though *latreuein* is also used of the service of the Gospel, Rom. 1: 9; and *leitourgein* (Acts 13: 2), though this is applied to the service of faith (Phil. 2: 17; Rom. 15: 16) and collection (2 Cor. 9: 12).

[2]Thus teaching is an ordained ministry (Acts 13: 1; 1 Cor. 12: 28; Eph. 4: 11; 1 Tim. 4: 13; 2 Tim. 1: 11) but also a gift freely given to individuals (Rom. 12: 7). Prophecy is a ministry (Acts 13: 1; 1 Cor. 12: 28; Eph. 4: 11) and a gift (Rom. 12: 6; 1 Cor. 12: 10; 13: 2; 14: 1 ff., 29 ff.). To be an evangelist is an order (Acts 21: 8; Eph. 4 11; 2 Tim. 4: 5—see also 1 Tim. 4: 14; 2 Tim. 1: 6) and a gift (Acts 8: 4). Similarly for exhortation (1 Tim. 4: 13, etc., on the one hand; Rom. 12: 8 on the other), speaking with tongues (Acts 2: 14; 1 Cor. 14: 18, etc. on the one hand; 1 Cor. 12: 10, etc., on the other).

with the spiritual gifts they have received, which they would forfeit if they refused the charge of the episcopate, having received them to use for the good of others, in imitation of Christ (see the passages quoted above, p. 45 seq.; St Thomas never separates the spiritual gifts of the individual from function, and what he wrote about the apostles [1] and the episcopate is significant in this connection.

However, let us note here a general scheme which we shall do well to keep in mind, for it throws light on many ecclesiological or pastoral problems. *Mission*, in its widest sense, is a *task* entrusted by the sender to his envoy, with resources sufficient for its accomplishment. These resources may either be simply and generally the spiritual gifts of Christian life, or particular gifts corresponding to election and vocation to the apostolate in its strict sense. In the first case, the mission is simply the moral responsibility to serve which is represented by Christian life as such or included in every grace from God; in the second case, the mission is election, call and mandate properly speaking, with the gifts of authority and power assignable to them, without prejudice to the spiritual gifts which accompany the formal mandate of the apostolate.

All the moral-ascetic values, with which some authors tend to identify the New Testament's remarks on the hierarchy as service, are equally to be found in an explanation of these passages which reaches to the very nature of Christian hierarchy: disinterestedness, seeking not one's own good but the good of others, seeking not

[1] Cf. A. Lemonnyer, 'Les Apôtres comme docteurs de la foi', in *Mélanges thomistes*, Le Saulchoir, 1923, pp. 153-73; N. Halligan, 'The Teaching of St Thomas Aquinas in regard to the Apostles'; *The American Eccles. Rev.*, 144 (1961) pp. 32-47.

one's own glory but the Master's, and so on.[1] Indeed it is here that these values find their deepest expression.

Human relationships 'in the Lord'

Everything springs from the fact that in Christianity relationships between men, or between the faithful and things, that is, the relationships which weave the fabric of our life on the horizontal plane of this world, are repeated or assumed into the vertical relationship of love which runs from God to us, and the vertical relationship of faith which runs from us to him.   This is what we see in St Paul, in his three types of relationship: with the outsider or the foreigner (Jew and Greek, or Greek and barbarian); between employer and employed, master and subordinate (slave-freeman); between man and woman. See Gal. 3: 28; Col. 3: 11; Philemon. The relation between slave and freeman, even between woman and man, is subordination. But if this human relationship is lived 'in the Lord', and so stems from him and is lived according to him, it ceases to be the natural relationship recognized by the civil code, sociology, economics or politics. It changes direction radically. It is no longer a relationship in two terms on the horizontal plane, one term opposed to the other, but in three terms, situated vertically. Will, providence and the gift of God travel through me as it were from top to bottom, and are relayed through me, without removing from me the sublime duty of willing acceptance. Everyone,

[1]See for instance St Thomas, *IV Sent.*, d. 24, q. 1, a. 1, qa 1 (=*Suppl.*, q. 34, a. 1, ad 1); *S.T.*, IIa IIae, q. 3, a. 2, ad 1 and 3; *In* 2 *Cor.*, c. 4, lect. 2.

according to his place in the earthly organism, whether of society or the Church (which, in this world, is a society, and not a pure communion of spiritual inwardness), bears the duty of care (*cura*) which God himself and his Christ have for their own, and in some measure entrust to us: 'Feed *my* sheep'.[1]

This duty is laid on every Christian, in a general way, with Christianity itself. Some receive it a second time, and in new fashion, when they are ordained to a position

[1]Fr L. Laberthonnière: 'Those who are called to command in this world, as well as those who are compelled to obey, no longer consider themselves as holding a position of superiority, a transcendant right to impose on others; but as having a function to exercise, a duty to fulfil towards them—in short, to be of use, not to use them, *ministrare* and not *ministrari*. This is because all have to strive towards the same spiritual goal, which is to bring about the communion of souls in God, and all must therefore practise the same duty of charity one towards another; so that in this perspective the distinction between those who command and those who obey has no meaning or scope except for the exterior and transitory order of this world'. *Etudes sur Descartes*, Vol. II, pp. 296 (quoted by L. Canet in the Foreword to his edition of *La notion chrétienne de l'autorité*, Paris, 1955, p. 40). Cf. above, p. 86, n. 2.

The passages of Fr Laberthonnière collected by L. Canet in this book are inspired by profound thinking which I have found stimulating. I feel, though, that his thinking falls short of the promise of his title, and so is not altogether satisfactory. It seems to me that Fr Laberthonnière sometimes excludes, or at least pretermits or belittles, any authority other than that attractive form exercised in sacrifice of *self* (see p. 16, end of note; p. 17, n. 1). All he sees is the moral aspect, or the aspect of the *education* of individuals, not the social aspect as such. He says, for instance, of those who command, that they 'have only a greater responsibility' (p. 34). This is dangerous, and may lead us to overlook the fact that their position of command gives them a title to responsibility other than the responsibility that every Christian has, and that this comprises authority in its strict sense. But it is true that essentially this authority gives them their place and order in the Christian condition, which consists entirely of service.

of authority. Authority is indeed a title in its own right, but the title is conferred within a general order of service and, in Christianity, has no existence outside this order. It is no longer defined basically as one man's ownership of or right over other men but *first* and fundamentally as a duty laid on us by God, as a responsibility and obligation entrusted to us:

> 'If I preach the Gospel, it is no glory to me; for a necessity lieth upon me ... If I do this thing willingly, I have a reward; but, if against my will, a dispensation is committed to me. What is my reward then? That preaching the Gospel I may deliver the gospel without charge' (1 Cor. 9: 16-18).

In the Gospel the dignity of the apostolate is linked with the person of Jesus and a mission received from him; and this is a clear indication that the dignity is given as a duty and obligation, not formally nor primarily as a right that belongs to the apostle.[1] Authority in the Gospel is a relationship of *sub et supra* (subordination and authority) within the general relationship of service, which is the necessary accompaniment of being a Christian. It is a duty, not a right:[2] *'nec imperio praesidere, sed ministerio:* to exercise authority not as a power,

[1] Cf. K. H. Rengstorf, art. *Apostolos*, in *T.W.N.T.*, vol. 1, pp. 426-7, trans. J. R. Coates, *Apostleship*, London, 1952, *Bible Key Words from Gerhard Kittel's Theol. Wb*.

[2] Cf. 'The New Middle Ages' in *The End of our Time*, trans. London, 1933, (though we reserve judgement on the position of the whole work): 'Power is a duty and not a right, and power is just only if one claims it not in one's own name, or the name of one's people, but in the name of God—the name of truth'. This passage expresses well the ethical aspect of the metaphysical argument that all power comes from God. Cf. Fr Heiler, *Evangelische Katholizität*, Munich, 1926, pp. 162 ff.

but as a service'.[1] As St Bernard says,[2] it is *cura* (what
one has responsibility for, but does not own), not
dominium (what one is master of).

Vocation to service

St Bernard saw the episcopate as consecration to a life
lived in the charity of Christ, in total and definitive self-
giving for the salvation of men.[3] Poverty and obedience
are the ascetic discipline of the religious; the bishop's
asceticism is self-dedication to all the battles and sacrifices of the apostolate, even to the point of giving his

[1]Tertullian, *De pudicitia*, 21, 6 (Oehler, p. 842). Cf. Origen, 'The
man who is called to the episcopate is not called to command, but
to the service of the whole Church' (*In Isaiam*, hom. 6, 1; *In Mat.*
comm. XVI, 8); G. Hocquard 'L'idéal du Pasteur d'âmes selon
saint Grégoire le Grand', in *La Tradition sacerdotale*, Le Puy, 1959, pp.
143-67; *Liber Mozarabicus sacrament.*, 'Inlatio' for the Feast of St
Martin: 'Quia sacerdotium, si recte ex Dei amore suscipitur, non est
dominatio putanda, sed servitus, et obseqium potius quam potestas'
(ed. Férotin, Paris, 1912, col. 398).

[2]St Bernard distinguishes between *dominium* and *ministerium* (*De
officio episcopi*, c. 1, 3; *P.L.*, 182, 812) or between *dominatus* and *cura*,
dominium and *dispensationis cura* (*Ep.* 14 to Honorius II: 182, 117; *Ep.*
117, 1, col. 281, 'sanctae suae Ecclesiae ministros, non dominos').
See in particular the *De Consideratione* addressed to Eugenius III, lib.
II, c. 6, n. 9, 'Impositum senserimus ministerium, non dominium
datum' (182, 747): n. 10, 'sonans tibi episcopi nomine non dominium,
sed officium' (747); n. 11, 'Forma apostolica haec est: dominatio
interdicitur, indicitur ministratio' (748); lib. III, c. 1, n. 1, 'Posses-
sionem et dominium cede huic (=Christo); tu curam illius habe'
(759); n. 2, 'Quid, inquis? non negas praeesse et dominari vetas?
Plane sic. Quasi non bene praesit, qui praeest in sollicitudine ...
Ita et sic praesis ut provideas, ut consulas, ut procures, ut serves.
Praesis ut prosis ... hoc est ut dispenses, non imperes' (759); c. 3
(764 ff.); lib. IV, c. 7, n. 23 (788).

[3]*De perf. vitae spir.*, c. 16 and 24; IIa IIae, q. 185, a. 4; *Quodl.* I,
q. 14, ad 2.

life, if need be.[1] This view of the episcopate is classic
in the Church, and its theme has been taken up and
developed in many treatises, especially since the Council
of Trent.[2] It expresses the Catholic ideal of the bishop. ✓
It is important that we should see in it not only the
ideal, but the *idea*, of the episcopate, pursuing this line
of thought until we arrive at the *notion* of the hierarchy
as service. This will lead us, if not to revise, at least to
define our ideas on the role of the priesthood and the
meaning of ordination, even on the vocation to the
priesthood, the first step on the road that leads through
seminary or training college to ordination. Before he becomes a priest, that is before he is ordained to a
directing post in the great Christian function of service,
a minister of the Church is a Christian. '*Vobis sum
episcopus, vobiscum christianus:* I am a bishop for your
sake but I am a Christian together with you.'[3]

The whole body is dedicated to the ministry and to
witness. Moreover, the whole body is consecrated, the
whole body is priestly: 1 Peter 2: 4 ff.; Ex. 19: 6. But
the body is organized according to the will of God, who
is the God not of dissension but of peace (1 Cor. 14: 33;
cf. 40). God calls some of his servants to become leaders
in service and to this leadership there are two titles, both
of which we must clearly understand: (1) the title of
one who knits together and organizes the service of all,

---

[1]*De perf.*, c. 16 to 18; IIa IIae, q. 185, a. 1 and 4. St Thomas makes
effective use of the most topical New Testament texts.

[2]The treatises of Bartholomew of the Martyrs and Louis of Gran-
ada were widely read. St Francis of Sales said, of his consecration as
bishop, 'God took me away from myself to take me to himself and
give me to the people, that I should no longer live save for him and
for them . . . '

[3]Cf. above, p. 54, n 2.

making it truly a service of the whole body, a communal ministry; (2) the title of a minister of the sacraments, of the gifts Christ makes to his people within the framework of the structures of the covenant, which cannot be reduced to the gifts he makes to men directly and personally. These two titles correspond to the two senses in which the priest is mediator : as an intermediary (the second title), and as the central point in whom and because of whom the charity of the faithful is knit together.

What we have said about the priest may equally be applied to the bishop, to the diocese or to the universal Church.

In this perspective, ordination is not only the hierarchical transmission of powers but also the consecration of the action by which the Church orders her charity and builds herself into a body in realization of the ministry which is concomitant with the state of being a Christian. To have a vocation to the priesthood, to prepare and present oneself for ordination, and eventually to receive consecration from the bishop, is to be called to Christian service in a more concentrated, more specific way, to be qualified to become a leader in this service and publicly to accept its character, having first accepted it in one's heart and striven to be worthy of it. It follows that the Church, that is the fellowship of all Christians, should play a large part in awakening the sense of vocation in training ministers, and finally in their ordination.[1] If we

[1]Abbé Germain Long-Hasselmans (cf. 21 February 1933) developed on these lines a very interesting application of his ideas on the priesthood. He had expressed his view in a paper read to the Congress of Recruitment to the Priesthood in 1926 (see B. Emonet, 'Les laïcs au Congrès du Recr. Sac. (Marseille, 3-5 Novembre 1926)' in *Etudes*, 189 (15 Dec., 1926), pp. 529-43), and in another and more synthetic

do not give all this, and the priesthood itself, its rightful place within the framework of the community of the faithful, we turn our backs on the meaning that the New Testament gives these realities.

So the whole Church bears the priesthood of those who, within her, are called to the ministry. She is wholly responsible for the idea that her hierarchical ministers have of the nature of their authority, and for the way in which they exercise it. If they are treated as potentates, they will become potentates. If they are deferred to with servility, it will be too easy for them to let their lives be ruined by the spirit of domination, which is very tenacious of life in the heathen that still survives in each one of us.

Authority in charity

Perhaps my account, however accurate in dealing with the New Testament texts, has left a certain uneasiness in the minds of some of my readers. Surely it has called into question the reality of the functions of the ministry as *hierarchical powers*. What is this authority whose very *nature* is service? Should we not revert to the conception that has been so summarily criticized: conceive the *nature* of authority as in the line of juridical power, '*secundum sub et supra*', and keep the 'mystique' of

lecture ('Le sacerdoce catholique'), given in 1930 and published in the *Bull. nat. des Instituteurs et Instit. cathol. de l'Enseignement public*, Oct. and Nov. 1930, pp. 30-6 and 79-84, republished in L. Giraud, *Une âme montante. L'abbé Long-Hasselmans* (1889-1933), Marseilles, 1937, pp. 259-73. The Abbé's synthesis, with documentation, and followed by critical notes appears in my paper : 'Un essai de théologie sur le sacerdoce cathol. La thèse de l'abbé Long-Hasselmans', in *Rev. Sc. rel.*, 25 (1951), pp. 187-99, 270-304.

service for the moral order of its *use*: in short, make it a question of personal virtue?

An authority most certainly does exist in the Church. The New Testament not only supposes or expressly affirms the existence of offices of authority, but often does so (and this is a fact to be carefully noted) actually in the context of its pronouncements on the hierarchy as service:

Matt. 18: 1 ff., on the need to become as little children, begins a chapter entirely devoted to the ministry, with vv. 15-18 on excommunication for sins of scandal.

In the very same logion in which he bids the apostles not to seek the first places, nor let themselves be called Rabbi, as is the way of the scribes and Pharisees, Jesus makes an exception for the authority of those who still sit on the chair of Moses: 'All things therefore whatsoever they shall say to you, observe and do' (Matt. 23: 2-3).

Luke 22: 25-7, on the greater being he who serves, is immediately followed by the passage concerning Peter, vv. 28-30.

John 13 begins with: 'The Father had given him all things into his hands.'

Cf. also above, p. 36, n. 1.

It would be just as mistaken to think that the ideal of loving service eliminated all 'power' as it would be dangerous to believe that authority in Christianity had reality or was defined *in the same way* as a juridical authority or a temporal power, with, as a kind of appendix, a moral obligation to exercise it in a spirit of service. Unfortunately this has too often been the case in

the history of the Church. In particular, each time that
the leaders of the Church have been involved in conflict
with secular powers and have translated their reaction
in terms of power against power: in Gregory VII's
struggle against the Emperor Henry IV;[1] during the
thirteenth century; in the struggles of bishops and popes
against kings; at the time of the great quarrel between
Boniface VIII and Philip the Fair, etc. Against this
background of purely juridical claims, even Gospel texts
on the pastorate have been used to justify the most
flagrant examples of constraint.[2] The way in which
biblical themes, which are fundamentally spiritual, have
been translated into juridical terms makes a deplorable
but highly instructive story.[3]

In a more general way, ecclesiology has too often
become simply a treatise on public ecclesiastical law. As
one result of this, the Church gave up applying to herself the New Testament themes of conversion, of the war
of the spirit against the flesh, etc. (and indeed, given
the conditions, this would have been impossible), though
the ecclesiological passages of the Fathers and the
liturgy are full of such applications. The Fathers never
separate the 'Church' and the community of the faithful; their ecclesiology is from beginning to end a
Christian anthropology. But obviously a juridical insti-

[1]Though we must of course note the context—a letter to Henry
IV—it is impossible not to feel that these words of Gregory VII are
much to be regretted: 'Non ultra putet (Henricus) sanctam ecclesiam
sibi subjectam ut ancillam, non praelatum ut dominam' (*Reg.* IV,
3; ed. Caspar, p. 298).

[2]Bellarmine and Sander (*De visibili Monarchia Ecclesiae*, Louvain,
1571) justify the use of torture by 'Pasce oves meas'! (cf. H. de Lubac
in *Rev. Sc. rel.*, 1932, p. 339, n. 3). Many other such examples could
be quoted.

[3]Cf. above, p. 61 ff.

4

tution, a power as such, or a legal structure, are not
called upon to be converted, nor to wage war against
the flesh, nor to do penance, nor to practise humility,
nor to forgive, nor to pray. . . . In short, the domain of
men and the Christian community was neglected for the
domain of *things*.

The fourteenth and fifteenth centuries saw a slight
reaction, but this was still within the juridical sphere, so
that to reinstate the pope in his evangelical place as
servant, there was erected a juridical theory of the *'caput
ministeriale'*; yet another theory of public law, contra-
dicting the one that went before it but of the same kind.
This was not the right reaction.

As one of you

We must get back to the true vision of the Gospel:
posts of authority in the Church do indeed exist; a real
jurisdictional power does exist, which the shepherds of
God's people receive from Christ in conformity with the
order which Christ willed and instituted (at least in its
essential lines). But this power exists only within the
structure of the fundamental religious relationship of the
Gospel, as an organizational element within the life given
to men by Christ, the one Lord and the one Head of
his Body, for which each is accountable to all the rest
according to the place and measure granted to him. So
there is never simply a relationship of subordination or
superiority, as in secular society, but always a loving
obedience to Christ, shaping the life of each with all and
for all, according to the position which the Lord has given
him in the Body. In this service, fundamentally identical

and coextensive with the fact of being a Christian, some
command and others obey: whether as leaders or as
simple members of the brotherhood, they are wholly en-
gaged in the service of Christ and their brethren. 'Doing
the truth in charity, even in all things grow up in him
who is the head, even Christ; from whom the whole body,
being compacted and fitly joined together, by what every
joint supplieth, according to the operation in the measure
of every part, maketh increase of the body, unto the
edifying of itself in charity' (Eph. 4: 15-16).

The relationship of superiority and subordination is
transformed by this. It is always of the Lord and in the
Lord. Not only in the sense, which we know only too well
from pronouncements designed to inculcate obedience,
that subordinates must consider their superiors as repre-
senting God himself and bearing in their person the
majesty of God, but in the sense that superiors and subordinates must serve God and men, confessing that all is
God's grace for all and through all, according to the
order in which God has placed each one of us. The
superior has indeed a position of authority, but in a
brotherly community of service: in the midst of the faithful he is 'quasi unus ex illis'.[1]

All this presupposes a radical conversion in us, not so
much to an ethical ideal of disinterestedness, for such an
ideal is only a consequence; but to God and Christ as

[1]In this sense *Si*, 32, 1 has often been quoted; cf. above, p. 34,
n. 3 (*Barnabas*, 4, 6): Council of Paris of 829, can. 23 (Mansi, XIV,
554); St Peter Damian, *Epist.* I, 12 (*P.L.*, 144, 217-18); Gregory
VIII, in the rule he gave to the community of canons regular he
founded at Benevento, his birthplace (no. 36, and quotation from
Matt. 20: 26-8: ed. P. Kehr, in *Miscellanea Fr. Ehrle*, vol. II, p. 273).
Cf. St Jerome, *Epist.* 82, 3, 'quasi unus in pluribus es, ut sis unum ex
pluribus' (*P.L.*, 22, 737; *ad Theophilum*, in 399).

the one absolute Lord: a conversion both *theistic* and *theological*. Much the same conversion as we must achieve if we are to 'use (this world) as though not using it'.[1] We must, in fact, sacrifice, abandon our human relationships in the form in which we receive them from the physical world of our first birth, which consist of two terms only: man and woman, master and servant; and we must receive them afresh from the hand of the Father as *Christian* relationships, and let them shape our lives 'in the Lord', so that we live in the unique relationship of love of God, of Christ, and of men as God and Christ love them, or, better, of the very love with which God and Christ love them. '*Sic Deus dilexit mundum.*' Only after such conversion can the relationship of authority exist and be lived in a Christian fashion.

[1]See 'Vie dans le monde et vie "dans le Seigneur" ', in *Les voies du Dieu vivant*, pp. 359-66. And W. Dirks, *La réponse des Moines*, Paris, pp. 58-62 and 114 ff.

II

Titles and Honours in the Church

A SHORT HISTORICAL STUDY

I

The Invasion of Legalism

If we go to the Fathers and the liturgy to discover what idea they had of the Church, we find ourselves in a climate which is not that of modern ecclesiology, at any rate not that of the ecclesiology predominant in the Schools between the end of the sixteenth century—or even the beginning of the fourteenth—and the renewal of our times. This scholastic ecclesiology was hardly more than the apologetic version of a treatise on public ecclesiastical law; it was entirely preoccupied with powers and rights. The Fathers and the liturgy speak of the Church in terms of the life and fellowship of the spirit, of the Holy City, of the war of the spirit waged against the flesh. They see her as symbolized or typified by the Patriarchs; by Rahab, the harlot saved by the scarlet cord tied in her window, which stands for faith in the blood of Christ; by Mary Magdalene, the unchaste one who became chaste; or by the Virgin Mary, blessed because she believed rather than because she bore Jesus Christ ... For to them the Church is made up of all who are converted to the Gospel. Their ecclesiology includes an anthropology and the means (sacraments, rules of life) by which men may live in communion with God in Jesus Christ.

A turning-point: the Gregorian reform

This form of ecclesiology persisted into the early Middle Ages. The great Schoolmen were in general still faithful to this tradition. But by the end of the eleventh century a new element was at work, a result of the Gregorian reform begun even before Gregory VII by Leo IX and Nicholas II. St Leo IX, with the advice and encouragement of Humbert of Moyenmoutier, and after him Gregory VII in particular, saw that the only possible way to effect the needful conversion of the clergy from the evils of the Nicolaitanism (incontinence) and even more from simony was to extricate the Church from her subjection to secular powers and, as a means to this end, to strengthen the authority and hence also the influence of the papacy. Gregory VII asked canonists, and in the first place St Peter Damian, to search out and assemble all the texts which could be used to support the strongest and most far-reaching form of papal authority and, under it, a wholesome order in the Church. Several canonical collections owe their existence to Gregory's appeal. It gave the decisive impetus to the establishment of canon law, alongside theology, as a discipline of university type in the schools, in the days when scholasticism was beginning; after St Yves of Chartres, Gratian of Bologna, with his *Decretum* (1140), was the classic exponent of the new science.

With Roland Bandinelli, who became Alexander III (1159-1181), canon law was firmly established on the pontifical throne. For two centuries thereafter, almost all popes were canonists, sometimes doctors *in utroque jure,* in both Roman law and ecclesiastical law.

This ascendancy of canon law was a development which the papacy found particularly useful in its conflict with the secular powers which continued throughout the 'age of faith': this was the age of 'Christendom', when ideally the two powers were as the two arms of one body, the two 'ministries' of a single Christian society. The main concern of the priesthood, or more accurately of the papacy, was to assert its rights in the face of a secular power ever ready to resist or encroach on them. *'Ecclesia non est ancilla, sed domina*—the Church is not a servant, but a mistress.'[1] Gregory VII's words were spoken in the context of the pope's struggle against the Emperor Henry IV. It must be understood in relation to this historical context (the need to shake off the tutelage, if not the domination, of the temporal power); but it is nevertheless a disturbing statement, being in substance the direct opposite of the Gospel principle: *non dominari, sed ministrare,* not to rule but to serve. Gregory VII and the Gregorians, for example St Anselm, made frequent use of the idea of the Church-Sponsa, the Bride: granted, this is definitely a mystical theme, but now directed—one might say slanted—towards an affirmation of the rights and authority of the 'Church', that is of clerics. As the Bride *of the Lord,* the Church is for all the faithful, but particularly for kings, 'Mother and Mistress'—mistress above all; her motherhood is invoked only to support her authority. Movements, even policies, have the strength of their 'mystique'. In this case the 'mystique' of an entire faith gave extraordinary strength

[1] Letter to the Bishops, Dukes and Counts of Germany, 3 September 1076: *Reg.* IV, 3, ed. E. Caspar, p. 298: 'Non ultra putet (the Emperor) sanctam ecclesiam sibi subiectam ut ancillam, sed preatam ut dominam'.

to the claims of the clergy to liberty, authority, and dominance. The story of St Thomas Becket and his 'murder in the cathedral' is an outstanding illustration of this.

The origins of the treatise on the Church

Ecclesiology began to be a subject treated in its own right with the works written in the thick of the struggle between the popes and the kings or emperors. The decisive moment in this connection was the conflict between Philip the Fair and Boniface VIII. In the space of a few months in 1300-1302 appeared the *De regimine christiano* of James of Viterbo, whose modern editor, H. X. Arquillière (1926), called it 'the first treatise on the Church'; the *De ecclesiastica potestate* of Giles of Rome; the *De potestate papali et regali* of John of Paris; and yet others.

Further, in the twenty years at the end of the thirteenth century and the first forty of the fourteenth, a legalistic form of reasoning overran whole sectors of theology. We feel the truth of this when we pass from reading St Thomas Aquinas or St Bonaventure, both of whom died in 1274 (one on his way to the Council of Lyons, the other while taking part in the Council), to those of Henry of Ghent (d. 1293), for instance, and above all William of Occam (d. 1349-50). Theological positions and conclusions were determined not so much by inherent reasons, arrived at after contemplative consideration of the deep inner nature of things, as by purely positive authorities, decretal texts the strength of whose coercive value was carefully assessed. On the subject of realities, an attitude based on consideration of normality yielded to a damaging approach, by way of exceptional cases, possible dispensations and the most far-fetched hypotheses. Nominalism was voluntarist; it was concerned with what God can do in extreme cases, regardless of what is reasonable (dialectic of the *potentia absoluta,* as opposed to the *potentia ordinata*); it resulted in a kind of positivism of free choice which encourages fideism in those who remain within the Church, or else a certain scepticism.

In theology, ethics, liturgy, etc., legalism raises the question of the most positive and strict conditions in which a thing can still bear its own name, be valid, satisfy an obligation. This attitude was especially prevalent and destructive in the liturgy.[1] Here it fostered an old material and markedly unspiritual instinct, which led men to concern themselves with the rite, the material and obligatory aspect of what was required of them, and not with the deeply personal involvement of the man who is not content merely to pay a debt but pledges his heart; interest was focused on the minimum legal

[1]The analytical spirit of scholasticism also played its part, when methodical distinctions, which can be so necessary and productive, began to lead to separation or dissociation. Even the great Cajetan (d. 1534) considered that a priest may say his breviary during the Kyrie of the sung mass, 'quoniam tunc non tam missa quam missae sollemnitas agitur' (*De valore orationum dictarum ab audientibus missam in die festo*: *Opuscula*, Antwerp 1612, fol. 118ᵛ). This example comes at the end of scholasticism. Here is one from its beginning: as a sequel to the heresy of Berengarius, and also as a result of the introduction of dialectics into theology, the exact moment of consecration in the Eucharist had to be determined. The canonist produced formulae of this kind: the words of the consecration are the *forma* or the *modus consecrandi*, the rest is *decor sacramenti* (cf. K. Goldammer, *Die eucharistische Epiklese in d. mittelalt. abendl. Frömmigkeit*, Bottrop, s.d. [1941], pp. 50-1, 63).

conditions of validity necessary for compliance with the law, at least with the letter of the law and authority, and not on the *meaning* of things. A similar attitude of mind, in matters of human conduct, resulted in the conception of casuistry as the art of getting round the law while respecting the letter of it.[1]

The spiritual degraded into 'things'

In all these cases we see living spiritual reality, inner quality and personal involvement degraded into *things*. A whole study could be devoted to this process of degradation in the pastoral letter, which can so easily degenerate into a series of recipes, a letter devoted to 'things'.... There is much, too, to be written about 'moralism', of which it has been said: 'Moralism begins at the point where the action is considered more important than the inspiration from which it springs.'[2] Good and evil are then detached, as it were, from the living subject which embraces them and which they qualify, and considered as things to be defined quantitatively by reference to completely external standards. Man is subordinated to the Sabbath, not the Sabbath to man. Regulation of a thing goes beyond the service necessary for good order, and becomes a value in itself. I have shown elsewhere[3] how the treatise of the Church took shape first in a climate of strife between the two powers

[1]See 'La casuistique de saint Paul', in *Sacerdoce et Laïcat*, Paris, ed. Cerf., 1962, pp. 65-89.

[2]A. N. Bertrand, *Témoins*, p. 59, quoted in A. Lalande, *Vocabulaire technique et critique de la Philosophie*, 8th ed., Paris, 1960, s.v.

[3]'Bull. d'Ecclésiologie', in *Rev. Sc. phil. théol.*, 31 (1947), pp. 77 ff: reproduced in *Sainte Eglise*, Paris, ed. Cerf., 1963, pp. 549 ff.

and their respective claims, then in a climate of refutation of successive heresies : the conciliarist heresy which refused to acknowledge the force of the papal element in the Church's divine constitution; the heresy of Wycliffe and Huss (Church of the Elect), which cast doubts on the visible nature of the Church and her hierarchical structure; the heresies of the Protestant reformers, who added to Wycliffe's a radical denial of the priesthood, the power of bishops and the pope, the sacraments, etc.; the heresies of the Gallicans and the episcopalist movement, which diminished the authority of the pope. All these heresies pointed in much the same direction. The reaction of orthodoxy followed their lead; it emphasized the aspects of the hierarchy, ending up by seeing the Church as practically nothing more than a society in which some commanded and the rest obeyed; but above all it exalted authority. It considered the Church from the viewpoint of her rights and the powers that made her a social structure; in a word, as a juridical subject of authority and rights.

Correspondingly, the relations of the Church with the world were seen chiefly from the legal standpoint, the main theme being the question of the two *Powers*. True, the deep inward life of the Church was constantly at work correcting and balancing these unilateral tendencies. On the one hand the Church was still the Church of the saints, of the life of the Gospel, of the love of God and man: 'Our Church is the Church of the saints' (G. Bernanos); she was still the Church of prayer, celebrating the liturgy and keeping safe within it, as in a living casket, the treasure of her deep-rooted tradition. On the other hand she was intensely apostolic and missionary, as she must always be for her full health.

Furthermore, it was very largely the hierarchy itself that effectively encouraged, by constant exhortation, the apostolate, the spirit of mission, charity and prayer, and kept safe the liturgy and the rules of holy life.

There is nothing whatever in my observations to suggest that the Church of charity and the Church of law are in any way opposed; all I have done is to explain historically how legalism has crept (as I am sure it has) into the outward appearances of the Church and sometimes into her practice. What I have criticized is a certain way of envisaging and presenting the Church; we must keep what truth it contains but we must denounce as an evil, from which the contemporary Church is, moreover, recovering remarkably quickly, its tyrannical and unworthy claims to ascendancy.

2

How the Church has Acquired its
"Appearance" of Privilege

NB

Before I approach the question of honours in the Church
(insignia and titles) historically, I must explain why I
feel it to be a matter of considerable importance. Honours
are by no means a negligible element in the Church's
visible structure, and this is not only theologically a very
important characteristic but also one of decisive importance in practical affairs. It is by the outward signs of the
Church, by what she is seen to be, that men know her
and through her are, or should be, brought to the Gospel,
led to God; or else they are estranged from her, repelled
or even turned towards some sort of religion of material
things, a system where sociological conduct predomi-
nates, rather than towards a personal religion with its
inherent spiritual demands. From this point of view,
then, the greatest importance attaches to everything that
makes the Church visible, everything by which it comes
into contact with men's lives, as their faces, looks, shape,
and outward trappings give us contact with our fellows;
it may be the wording of a poster, a notice, a parish
magazine, or more likely a form of ornamentation or
celebration . . . the look of the priest, his manner or turn
of speech, the way he lives—and the same applies to a

nun, or any cleric. These are minor everyday elements in the Church's visible form, in her role as the parable of the kingdom of God or the sacrament of the Gospel, but they have their significance none the less and it may be decisive. The man in the street comes across the leaders and dignitaries of the Church less frequently; but the image of the Church they present is obviously just as important—even more important, as their appearances are likely to be more memorable.

On the other hand our outward circumstances, the setting in which we live our lives, the way we are customarily treated, the image of ourselves and our office which we see reflected in all these, are powerful factors in moulding our ideas and attitude. Can we as a rule enjoy privileges without coming to feel they are rights, or live in some degree of luxury without forming certain habits, be honoured, flattered, treated with solemn and brilliant ceremonial, without setting ourselves morally on a pedestal? Can we always command and judge, receive men as petitioners, eager with their compliments, without getting into the habit of not really listening? In short, if we are always attended by thurifers, can we avoid acquiring a liking for incense?

Insignia and titles

Among the aspects of privilege in the Church's image in the world today, I shall confine myself here to insignia and titles. First because I must set myself a limit; a study of all that goes to make the Church's visible aspect would be too extensive. And then because insignia and titles, especially insignia, have been the subject of a great many studies in the last thirty years, especially by German historians, who are very much alive (sometimes excessively so) to what concerns the Holy Roman Empire and, in consequence, to this aspect of ecclesiastical realities.[1]

Modern historians of apostolic and primitive Christianity reject the idea that the first Christian communities existed without any definite juridical organization. The historical evidence—the epistles, the Acts, the letters of St Clement of Rome, and of St Ignatius of Antioch ('Theophorus'), the Epistle and the Martyrdom of St Polycarp, finally the *Didache* whose date and prove-

---

[1]Chief studies: E. Muntz, *La tiare pontificale du VIIIe au XIVe siècle*, Paris, 1898; E. Wüscher-Bacchi, 'Ursprung der päpstlichen Tiara unde der bischöflichen Mitra', in *Röm. Quartalsch.*, 13 (1899), pp. 77-108; K. von Amira, *Der Stab in der germanischen Rechtssymbolik*, Munich, 1908; J. Braun, *Die liturgische Gewendung*, Fribourg, 1914; S. Alföldi, *Die Ausgestaltung des monarchischen Zeremonielles am römischen Kaiserhofe*: *Mitteilungen des deutschen archäolog. Instituts, Römische Abt.*, 49 (1934), pp. 3 ff. and 50 (1950); G. Ladner, 'Die Statue Bonifaz's VIII. und die Entstehung der dreifachen gekrönten Tiara', in *Röm. Quartalsch.*, 42 (1934), pp. 35-69; O. Treitinger, *Die Oströmischen Kaiser u. Reichsidee*, Jena, 1938; Th. Klauser, *Der Ursprung der bischöflichen Insignien u. Ehrenrechte*, Bonn, 1948 (reviewed by S. Mazzarino, in *Jura*, 7 [1956], pp. 349-52); E. Eichmann, *Weihe und Krönung des Papstes im Mittelalter*, Munich, 1951; W. Ullmann, *The Growth of Papal Government in the Middle Ages*, London, 1955, ch. X, pp. 310-43; H. U. Instinsky, *Bischofstuhl u. Kaiserthron*, Munich, 1955; D. P. Salmon, *Etude sur les Insignes du Pontife dans le rite romain, Hist. et Liturgie*, Rome, 1955; id., 'Aux origines de la Crosse des évêques', in *Mél. M. Andrieu*, Strasbourg, 1956, pp. 373-83; P. E. Schramm, *Herrschaftszeichen u. Staatssymbolik*, Stuttgart, 3 vols., 1954-6; id., *Kaiser Friedrich II. Herrschaftszeichen . . .*, 1955; *Herrschaftszeichen*, Göttingen, 1958; id., 'Sacerdotium-Regnum im Austausch ihrer Vorrechte. Eine Skizze der Entwicklung zur Beleuchtung des "Dictatus Papae" Gregors VII.', in *Studi Gregoriani*, II, Rome, 1947, pp. 303-457; id. *Sphaira, Globus, Reichsapfel, Wanderung u. Wandlung eines Herrschaftszeichens von Caesar bis zu Elisabeth II*, 1958; Ph. Hofmeister, *Mitra und Stab der wirklichen Prälaten ohne bischöflichen Character*, Amsterdam, 1962.

nance are so elusive—all show a very real authority at
the head of the Churches. But this was an authority of
leaders outstanding in spiritual gifts, of leaders of the
spiritual life; the juridical domain did not extend to
matters of spiritual warfare, nor the ecclesiological to the
affairs of man as a spiritual and Christian being. The
prestige of the leaders of God's people stood high, but
we have no evidence that they used external means to
support it.

And yet it is only human to use such means. Even
before the Peace of Constantine we see signs of a
tendency to seek prestige through external, honorific
distinctions. Paul of Samosata had a high throne set up
for himself, and the bishops had to appeal to the
Emperor Aurelian (a pagan!) before they could dispossess
him of his see of Antioch.[1] But in the new situation
created by Constantine external means of prestige were
introduced as the result not of men's natural instincts
alone but of the new conditions imposed on the Church
within the Empire.

The Church within the Empire

Though we must not lay all evils at the door of Constantine the Great, we must recognize the influence of
his policy on conditions of life in the Church. Hence-

[1] See Eusebius, H. E., VII, 30, 9 (for the throne, but Paul of S.
sought a good many other signs of authority as well!) and 30, 19
for the appeal to Aurelian (*Sources chr.*, 41, 1955, pp. 216, 219). In
his commentary on Matt. 16: 25, Origen speaks of leaders of the
people of God, especially in large towns, who would not suffer even
the most authentic disciples of Jesus to address them on an equal
footing.

forward the Church was *within the Empire*, as Optatus of Milevis wrote about 370.[1] The Bishop of Milevis, confronted with the Donatist schism, resorted to the logic of the age which began with Constantine; he claimed recourse to force and to State compulsion to be justifiable, in order to crush stubborn dissentients and those who foment sedition.[2]

Under Constantine and after his time, in the framework of an officially Christian Empire, the bishops were given privileges and honours. They ranked in the Order of the *Illustri* and took their place in the hierarchy of the State. Men who were in hiding the very day before, some bearing the marks of tortures undergone during the persecution, travelled to the Council of Nicaea (325) by the Imperial post, and as they came out of the Council were received in the Imperial palace at Constantinople, honoured by the highest officials. 'It felt,' wrote Eusebius, 'as if we were transported into the Kingdom of God. . . .'[3]

It is difficult to be sure of the exact origin of different insignia and to say definitely that they began in a borrowing from the official dress of the great Imperial officers. But this does seem to have been the case with the *pallium*, which made its appearance in both East and

[1] III, 3; *P.L.*, 11, 900 B; CSEL, 26, p. 74, 3.

[2] The Donatists, on the other hand, who were certainly not models of all the virtues and were perfectly prepared, if not to use violence themselves, at least to use the support of their allies', rejected the situation which the Peace of Constantine created, and claimed to be the Church of the poor; see my general introduction to *Bibl. augustinienne. Oeuvres de saint Augustin, Traités antidonatistes*, Paris, 1963, pp. 37 ff. and 35, n. 2.

[3] *Vita Constantini*, III, 21. On the bishops as *illustri*, of whom there were five classes, cf. P. Salmon, *Etudes . . .* , pp. 20-1.

West in the fifth century; and with the *stola* and the
pontifical shoes, which date from the same period and
were the insignia of high officials.[1] Certainly, priests
were put on their guard against the dangers of seculari-
zation and loss of savour that the favours of the political
authorities represented for Christianity and the Church.[2]
But how could such favours be avoided? The privileges[3]
accorded to the clergy could easily be justified by the
argument that they served spiritual and heavenly realities far higher than all the earthly realities that were
honoured. Moreover, the liturgy, hitherto sober and
functional, content to express the spiritual worship of the
faith in acts of acceptance of God's gift and of thanks-
giving, now began to develop a splendid ceremonial,
many of its elements being borrowed from that of the
Court: processions, sumptuous vestments, gold furnishings and vessels—all the rich display of liturgical ceremonies . . .

[1]Klauser, *op. cit.*, pp. 18 ff.; Salmon, *Etude* . . . , pp. 21-3.

[2]Evidence for this in: Origen, in 244 ff., *Comm. in Mat.* XVII, 24
(*GCS, Orig. Werke*, I, p. 625); *In Jerem.*, hom. 4, 3: 'Once there were
men of faith, when noble martyrdom was common . . . ' Eusebius
noted how a state of well-being, the result of peace and imperial
favour, induced a condition of indolence in which internal divisions
flourished (H.E., VIII, 1; *Sources chr.*, 55, Paris, 1958, pp. 3-6);
St Ambrose, *Exp. in Ps.* 118, sermo 11, n. 21-2; St Gregory Nazianus,
Carm. II, 1, *De Seipso*, XI: *De vita sua* 20 ff. (*P.G.*, 37, 1031); St
Jerome, *Vita Malchi Monachi*, 1: 'postquam ad christianos principes
venerit, potentia quidem et divitiis maior, sed virtutibus minor facta
est (Ecclesia)' (*P.L.*, 23, 55: c. 390); St Augustine, *En. in Ps.* 7, 9
(*P.L.*, 36, 103: 'postquam in tanto culmine nomen coepit esse christ-
ianum, crevit hypcrisis, id est simulatio, eorum scilicet qui nomine
christiano malunt hominibus placere quam Deo . . . '); *Ps.* 30 sermo
2, 6 (col. 242-3); and see my *Intro.* quoted above (p. 115 n. 2), p. 40;
Vraie et fausse réforme dans l'Eglise, Paris, 1950, p. 169.

[3]Cf. J. Gaudemet, *L'Eglise dans l'Empire romain* (*IVᵉ-Vᵉ siècles*)
(*Hist. du Droit et des Inst. de l'Egl. en Occident*, III), Paris, 1958.

It became natural to use a vocabulary originating in the Imperial or political sphere in speaking of the realities of Christianity: the Gospel is a 'law'; God is the supreme Emperor of the world, and the angels his ministers; Peter and Paul are the *principes* (princes) or *senatores mundi* (high dignitaries of the world).[1]

So there came to be added to the sacred things of God himself, which are the realities at work in the history of salvation, which men gladly receive and use, the sacred things of a ceremonial of great beauty, rich in symbols that the contemplative soul will never exhaust, to its unfailing joy. To give one example: in primitive days churches were consecrated only by the congregation's habitual use, and the fact of a first eucharist celebrated on the altar;[2] but from the fourth century there was introduced a sanctification and consecration of the altar before this first celebration, in a rite taken from the Old Testament.[3] In our day the consecration of churches has developed into a ceremony that is full of wonderful symbolism, but complicated and spectacular, involving a ritual consecration of *things*, which tends to swamp the sanctification of the *ecclesia* by living faith.

[1]See my article on 'Le thème du "don de la Loi" dons l'art paléochrétien', in *Nouv. Rev. théol.*, 84 (1962), pp. 915-33; Ch. Pietri 'Concordia Apostolorum et Renovatio Urbis (culte des martyrs et propagande pontificale)', in *Mélanges d'Archéol. et d'Hist.*, 73 (1961), pp. 275-322 (pp. 289 ff.).

[2]See P. Battifol, 'La dédicace des églises. Dédicace païenne et dédicace chrétienne', in *Rev. Sc. phil. théol.*, 28 (1939), pp. 58-70.

[3]A. G. Martimort, *L'Eglise en prière. Introd. à la Liturgie*, Paris, 1961, pp. 179 ff.; J. des Graviers, 'La dédicace des lieux de culte aux Ve et VIe siècles', in *l'Année canonique*, 7, 1960 (ed. 1962), pp. 107-25.

Vestiges of feudalism

So the history whose great epochs and main elements
I am trying to define reached its first peak in the centuries
which saw the Peace of Constantine and the establishment of the legislative code of the Most Christian
Empire (Theodosius), followed by the conversion of barbarian princes and the setting up of Christian kingdoms.
Its second great period, in the West, came at the end of
the Merovingian and into the Carolingian age. Germanic
influence, very pronounced at that time, led to the
meaning of everything that was done being translated
into gestures, by handing over and touching a significant
object: for example, to pledge obedience one put one's
hands between the hands of a superior; investiture involved the tradition of the instruments or insignia. It is
in Visigothic Spain in the seventh century, in Gaul in
the eighth, that we first find the crozier, or at least the
pastoral staff (*baculus, virga*); this was unknown in
Rome before the eleventh century, although the Bishop
of Rome appears in the eighth century bearing a
ferula (pastoral staff). The episcopal ring appears in the
eighth century in Spain and Gaul.[1]

Much more important at this time was the revival of
the idea, the prestige, and the ideal of the Empire and
Rome as a reality or myth of empire. Possibly it sprang
from the need to compete with Byzantium, whence
genuflexion (*proskunesis*) and the kissing of feet were
borrowed at that time;[2] possibly from the desire to make

[1] Cf. Klauser, *op cit.*, pp. 17 ff.; Salmon, *Etude*, p. 24.
[2] See W. Ullmann, *op. cit*, p. 315, n. 4.

a stand against Frankish influence, at once protective
and intrusive. Historians are still arguing over the date,
place of composition, and exact intention of the all too
famous 'Donation of Constantine'. But however important these details may be, they do not affect the results
that concern us here: all things considered, the legendary 'Donation', which was almost everywhere accepted
as authentic down to the time of the humanists (Lorenzo
Valla), and was still invoked by some nineteenth-century
ultra-montanists, had considerable influence on the
tendency to model the realities of the Church on the
realities of the Empire. We will not concern ourselves
here with the ideological myth of an Empire which was
to endure for ever, and of one universal republic united
under the aegis of some supreme power.[1] It was thought
that Constantine had been warned by a vision of the
apostles Peter and Paul to seek out Pope Sylvester, and
had been baptized and cured of leprosy by him. He had
then resolved to honour the pope, vicar of the Son of
God on earth, he who occupied the place of the prince
of apostles, by bestowing on him the authority and
honours of the imperial dignity.[2] The rest of the document deals with the Lateran Church, *caput et vertex*
(head and pinnacle) of all churches (No. 13 in Mirbt's
edition), the Lateran Palace (No. 14), and then the
imperial insignia conceded to the pope: the diadem, the

[1] The myth was active in the East in the idea of Constantinople—
Second Rome— and then of Moscow—Third Rome—an idea which
still influences the world today! In a more or less secular form, it
reappears to some extent in all the myths of unity of the Christian
world, or just of the world: cf. E. Gilson, *Les métamorphoses de la Cité de
Dieu*, Louvain and Paris, 1952.

[2] Text in C. Mirbt, *Quellen zur Geschichte des Papsttums*, no. 228,
pp. 107-112.

phrygium (but it is said that Sylvester would accept
only the round white mitre, the *phrygium,* and not the
diadem), the shoulder scarf, the purple cloak (*chlamys*),
the red tunic—in short, all the adornments of an
Emperor, even down to the sceptre; it is clear from the
text that the imperial character of these insignia was well
understood (Nos. 14, 16). The pope, like the emperor,
was to have his senate and his legates; there are of course
biblical antecedents for these (councils, messengers), but
they make their appearance here as institutions modelled
on those of the Empire (No. 15). The emperor was to
exercise the *officium statoris* (the office of squire) as Constantine did, leading on foot the horse on which the Pope
rode. There follows the well-known gift of lands '*ad
imitationem Imperii nostri,* on the model of our Empire'
(No. 17), and finally the statement that Constantine has seen fit to transfer his capital to the East
(No. 18).

These authorizations had far-reaching effect. Not that
the popes themselves invoked the legendary Donation—
that would have been an admission that they owed something to the concession of a secular power, and they were
conscious that they held their authority by right of the
Gospel and by divine right itself. But the imperial idea,
upheld by all the concrete apparatus of insignia, titles,
the organization of the Roman court and its services,
in a word, all the ceremonial, was largely responsible
for the development of papal claims and the day to day
administration of the Church along imperial lines.[1]
Representations, images, myths, were all those of a

[1] Cf. J. B. Saegmüller, 'Die Idee von der Kirche als Imperium
Romanum im kanonischen Recht', in *Theol. Quartalsch.,* 80 (1928),
pp. 50-80.

monarchy on the imperial model. So were all the
appendages of prestige. In more than one case, tracing
these external signs of sovereignty back through history,
we are led beyond Byzantium to the time of the hellenistic monarchy, and it even seems that this derived
several of its insignia from Persia.[1]

The Church lives in time. The structures, ideas and
means of action existing in an historical setting at a
given moment largely condition the outward forms of
her life and action. For more than half a millennium the
Church lived among feudal structures, and from this
time date many of the texts on which Catholic theology
has been built up. Feudalism was a social system determined by two facts: (1) every man was bound to the
land, and his condition was determined by that of the
land on which he was born and lived; and (2) lands were
not equal in value.

Under the feudal system, a man was always bound to
the land, and the land transmitted its value to the man
living on it; he was lord, landowner and master, or vassal
and tenant, according to whether he possessed the land
or held it from another in return for certain duties or
services. These relations extended hierarchically from
top to bottom of society, from the king who was no one's
dependant but to whom the lords were enfeoffed, down
to the poor man who was simply a dependant, the
liegeman of a lord who was himself the liegeman of his

---

[1] C. Toumanoff gives as references (*Theolog. Studies*, 7 (1946), p.
216, n. 4): J. B. Bury, *The Constitution of the Later Roman Empire*,
Cambridge, 1910; L. Bréhier, 'L'origine des titres impériaux à
Byzance', in *Byzantin. Zeitsch.*, 15 (1905), pp. 162-77; J. Maurice,
'Les Pharaons romains', in *Byzantion*, 12 (1937), pp. 71-103; E.
Kornemann, 'Die römische Kaiserzeit', in A. Gerke—E. Norden,
Einleitung in die Altertumswiss., 2nd ed., 1914, III, App. 4.

suzerain. The Church too was subject to this system. Although her lands were gradually freed and made directly subject to the king, she too had her vassals and tenants; she too had a hierarchy of nobles, linked with the lands attached to certain offices; she had bishops who were princes or counts,[1] she had chapters and abbeys varying in degree of dignity. In this medieval, hierarchical world a man's quality, which included his duties and rights, his obligations and privileges, was expressed not only in titles and insignia but in a manner of living, a style of dress. Today, when things of quality can be bought and are available to anyone who can pay for them, anyone can wear any clothes. But dress proper to a calling or condition still persists, even though the feudal system has long since been swept away, and to some extent maintains a distinction of orders: e.g., in army and clergy, and in each uniforms and insignia of rank. No doubt this will be so for a long time yet.

It is important for our discussion to recognize that the feudal age has left traces behind it. We can attach what importance we like to them. *Dominus* carries little weight in 'Dom' So-and-so, and Monsignor is no less inoffensive. Titles such as 'my Lord Bishop' are, or should be, the province of local history societies, together with old titles vested in chapters, which only rarely survive nowadays and are reflected in a few details of costume. Generally speaking, feudalism is a thing of the past. And yet surely there still clings about bishops and the Curia an aura of feudal privilege expressed in dress,

---

[1]A certain Archbishop of Rouen said that he had a wife, not as Archbishop of Rouen, but as Count of Evreux.

insignia, 'retinue',[1] the deference paid to them,[2] all the trappings of heraldry? The economic and social structures of feudalism have disappeared, but some vestiges still remain on the surface, and occasionally titles and privileges still have some real value : but they are mainly external, part and parcel of the nature of man in his physical state.

Constantine or Peter?

The third great period of extensive borrowings of titles and insignia from the powers of this world was during the reforming pontificate of St Gregory VII (1073-1085). The facts are all before us, in the chronicles, the *Ordines Romani* describing the ceremonies of the pope's coronation and enthronement, the *realia,* the monuments that have survived to our days. But we also have most explicit statements : in particular the *Dictatus Papae,* the list of propositions drawn up by Gregory VII in 1075, which represent the legal basis of the claims he wished to see maintained. Here are some of them : '*Quod solus (Papa) possit uti imperialibus insigniis.* Only

---

[1]But there is no comparison between this and the retinue of the feudal bishops of the Middle Ages, especially of the waning Middle Ages which, as Huizinga has pointed out, exaggerated all the medieval characteristics and shortcomings. Here are some figures: at the Third Lateran Council, 1179, prelates arrived with 20 to 30 horses; at the Council of Constance, the Archbishop of Mainz had a retinue of 452, and the Archbishop of Salzburg, 260; at the Council of Trent, Cardinal Ercole Gonzaga had a retinue of 160, and Cardinal Alexander Farnese (the future Paul III) 360 servants, but the average per prelate was nine.

[2]Kissing the hand, genuflexion; for popes, kissing the feet (the old *proskunesis* of Byzantium, implying prostration), censing.

the Pope is entitled to use the imperial insignia';[1] the corresponding passage in the Avranches manuscript reads: '*Soli Papae licet in processionibus insigne quod vocatur regnum portare cum reliquo paratu imperiali.* Only the Pope may wear in processions the insignia known as the tiara, or the rest of the imperial insignia' (c. 10). What were these insignia? First the red cloak and the red shoes, introduced as early as the eighth century. Then the tiara, *corona* or *regnum,* a triple-ringed mitre distinct from the ordinary mitre (in the mid-eleventh century the word *mitra* began to be used for the old *phrygium*), which was called the *tiara* from the end of the eleventh century onwards.[2] The Church was well aware that it was imitating the Empire or the structure of Ancient Rome. It was then that the cardinals, who elected the pope without any intervention of laymen, were assimilated to the senate of the Church, and that the word *Curia* was introduced to designate the services of the pontifical administration and the pope's entourage;[3] soon afterwards St Bernard repudiated the term as

[1]Dict. 8; ed. Caspar, *Reg.*, p. 204.

[2]See the studies quoted above, p. 113, n. 1, of Schramm (*Studi Greg.*), and Ullmann (p. 310 ff.); cf. H. Leclercq, art. 'Tiare', in *Dict. Arch. chr. Lit.*, XV, col 2292-8. I quote from St Bruno of Segni (XI century): 'Summus autem Pontifex propter haec et regnum portat (sic enim vocatur) et purpura utitur, non pro significatione, ut puto, sed quia Constantinus imperator olim beato Silvestro omnia Romani imperii insignia tradidit unde in magnis processionibus omnis ille apparatus Pontifici exhibetur, qui quondam imperatoribus fieri solebat' (*P.L.*, 165, 1108).

[3]This is what St Peter Damian, himself a cardinal, says of the College of Cardinals: 'Romana Ecclesia, quae sedes est Apostolorum, antiquam debet imitari Curiam Romanorum: The Roman Church, which is the seat of the Apostles, should imitate the old Roman Senate' (Opusc. 31, *Contra philargyrium*, c. 7 (*P.L.*, 145, 540).

a neologism and an indication that secular usages were invading the Church.[1]

It was St Bernard too who wrote to his former subordinate Eugenius III (pope from 1145 to 1153): 'When the pope, clad in silk, covered with gold and jewels, rides out on his white horse, escorted by soldiers and servants, he looks more like Constantine's successor than St Peter's.'[2] St Bernard likewise censured the pomp which surrounded bishops, covered with red-dyed ermine 'called gules'[3]; they look like young brides on their wedding-day![4] And he upbraided the abbots who had just then obtained from the Holy See the right to wear mitre, ring and sandals, like the bishops.[5]

The fourth epoch in the history whose most significant stages we are reviewing was the reign of Boniface VIII (1294-1303)—a man whose character allows of conflicting interpretations. It was he who introduced the triple-crowned tiara, the *triregnum*,[6] which those attending the Council might see on the head of St Peter's statue in the majestic nave of the Vatican Basilica. The shape of the tiara, rising from a wide base to a single point at the top, was an apt expression of the idea of pontifical monarchy and a quasi-pyramidal concept of the

[1]See my paper, 'L'ecclésiologie de saint Bernard', in *Saint Bernard théoligien*: *Anal. S. Ord. Cisterc.*, 9 (1953), pp. 136-90.

[2]St. Bernard, *De Consideratione*, IV, 3, 6 (*P.L.*, 182, 776 A).

[3]*Tract. de moribus et off. episc.*, 2, 4 (*P.L.*, 182, 813 B).

[4]*In Cant.* sermo 77, 1 (*P.L.*, 183, 1155 D—1156A).

[5]*Tr. de moribus et off. episc.*, 9, 36 (182, 832 CD). Cf. P. Salmon, *Etude*, pp. 50 ff.; the ring was widely used at the end of the twelfth century, p. 54; but the adoption or concession of *pontificalia* for Abbots reached its peak in the fourteenth, pp. 72 ff.

[6]Cf. G. Ladner, 'Die Statue Bonifaz' VIII in der Lateran Basilika u. die Entstehung der dreifachen gekrönten Tiara', in *Röm. Quartalsch.*, 42 (1934), pp. 35-69.

Church.[1] The triple-crowned tiara symbolizes the unity of the Church extending over a united world: the true ecumenical emperor is the pope, he who rules over the unity of the universe.[2] It was inevitable that conflict should arise between the old imperial idea of universal unity under a single crowned head, and the papal idea, which based its claim to be the means of effecting this grandiose programme on the most sacred grounds. But in the course of their rivalry both empire and papacy borrowed the other's ideological themes, translated into physical or symbolic terms.

To the pomp of Renaissance times we owe many of the forms of ceremonial and protocol used today by the papal court.

Borrowing on both sides continued. Nowadays abuse of the printed word, and notably journalism, has atrociously weakened the meaning of language, and only the vocabulary of religion still keeps its force and prestige. So we resort to it when we want to express things on a certain level of intensity or dignity. The order of religion still has great prestige. . . . We speak of a sufferer as a martyr to his illness, medicine or teaching is a *vocation* and so on.[3] But the Church also borrows terms: after taking over the Byzantine title of 'Eminence',[4] she has in our own time adopted the title of

[1]Cf. the document *Non ponant laici*, early in 1302, in Scholz, *Unbekannte kirchenpolitische Streitschriften aus d. Zeit Ludwigs d. Bayern*, Rome, 1911, pp. 474-5.

[2]See J. Leclerq, *Jean de Paris et l'ecclésiologie du XIIIᵉ siècle*, Paris, 1942, pp. 59 (n. 5) ff.

[3]*L'Est républicain* of 5 Jan. 1959: 'Noon on 8 January—a historic moment: de Gaulle will be *consecrated* President of the Republic to the sound of a 101-gun salute'.

[4]Cf. M. Noirot, in *Catholicisme*, IV., col 54-5.

'Excellency', so that no less honour may be imputed to
her bishops than Mussolini allowed his prefects. . . .[1]

'Shake off the dust of the empire'

The modern state has reviewed and to a great extent
rejected its borrowings from the Church, and that ad-
mixture of sacred or religious elements which for
centuries it not only admitted but sought out. The
tendency of modern society is to build on reason, not on
religion.[2] Has the Church likewise reviewed the profane
elements, imperial, feudal or courtly, which for so long
she not only tolerated but actively encouraged? The
Holy Roman Empire no longer exists, but there still
remain in the Church many titles and insignia, many
elements of ceremonial and so of her visible aspect,
borrowed at some time from the dazzling imperial
splendour. Surely it is high time, and surely it would be
to everyone's advantage, 'to shake off the dust of the
Empire that has gathered since Constantine's day on the
throne of St Peter.' Those words were spoken by John
XXIII.

In time past, these trappings, this whole system of
symbols, developed a meaning which in that social tradition was readily understandable even to the humblest.

[1]See the decree of the Congregation of Ceremonial, 31 Dec. 1930:
Acta Ap. Sedis, 1931, p. 22; *Catholicisme*, V, col. 188.

[2]Chateaubriand, art. of 5 July 1824, quoted in *Mémoires d'Outre-
tombe*, 3e partie, 2e époque, 1. VI, para. 8: 'Time has reduced this
monarchy to its reality. The age of fictions is over for politics; there
can no longer be a government based on adoration, worship and
mystery: everyone knows his rights, nothing is possible beyond the
boundaries of reason, and everything—even favour, that last illusion
of absolute monarchies—is weighed and assessed today'.

Such is no longer the case today. In one sense this is a good thing, since it makes them relatively inoffensive. Nevertheless, even if their exact import is no longer clearly apparent, they still carry a general implication of external, wordly, feudal, imperial prestige. Though they no longer have definite positive value, they have the general value of symbols, and what they express is not that evangelical service to which the very men who bear these insignia and titles of a different world are dedicated (often with very great fervour). There has been much talk recently of 'countersigns'. We must ask ourselves, in the light of the Gospel, what are the consequences or effects of all these signs of prestige.

It is not an easy problem. We must have signs and insignia. When the highest office is borne by a man too much like other men, perhaps even less well-favoured or well-endowed than they, his person must, as it were, be set free from the too personal, too human limits of his individuality, and in some way exalted and honoured by the badges of his dignity. The possibilities in this direction are limited—a few fabrics, a few colours, forms of honorific headgear or long flowing garments to add splendour and nobility. . . . Again, it must be acknowledged that the Church has in general succeeded in creating honorific forms of great and compelling beauty. Fr Romane-Musculus recently argued in favour of an official dress which gives a man impersonality and focuses attention on his office;[1] but he was talking of *liturgical* vestments. I am myself unreservedly in favour not only of liturgical vestments, but of a dress expressing state or office, of insignia interpreting the dignity and

[1]'Le vêtement liturgique dans l'Eglise réformée', in *Verbum Caro*, no. 20, 1951, pp. 179-84.

inspiring respect for it. But all this must be (1) intelligible, and more in keeping with the world we live in; (2) less weighted, or over-weighted, with history to the point where certain things need research and erudite footnotes to explain them; (3) always commensurate with the office, which, in the last resort, means with service; and that implies a drastic revision of everything stemming from dignities, situations and sometimes pretentions which are secular and political and have very little to do with the Gospel.

It is not easy to say exactly what we should like to see changed. Perhaps indeed we ought not to try to change things too quickly. We must state the problem, collect information that will throw light on the admitted facts, foster a healthy insistence on the truth of the Gospel in this sphere as in others, and then leave the Christian people and their priests to find valid ways to meet this need for truth and authenticity. I shall end this contribution, which has been on the level of an historical investigation and a few questions of principle, by suggesting some reflexions of greater scope than the particular problem of titles and insignia we have broached here.

In antiquity and the middle ages men had few images of beauty and luxury and splendour apart from those of temples and palaces, priests and kings. The need for something that went beyond the commonplace, something that kindled and sustained the imagination, found almost its only satisfaction in the splendid pageantry of princes and religious ceremonies, and in the legends of saints, which did much to meet this human need for something more than the humdrum daily round. When the Russians, who were still not highly civilized, went to Byzantium and witnessed the splendid Greek liturgy, they thought themselves in heaven: 'We knew not if we were in heaven or on earth, for there is no such spectacle on earth, nor any such beauty.'[1]

Today, pomp and splendour can be found outside the churches. These elements undoubtedly contribute to the attraction of dance-halls and cinemas. It is true, though, that by comparison church ceremonies have a dignity, perfection and beauty, an emotional quality of reverence, that cannot be equalled by any other ceremonial. A friend who is very 'lay', even a little anticlerical, said to me once: 'It is only in church nowadays that ceremony can be properly performed.'

Above all, our imagination today has more to feed on than the mysteries of the liturgy or the legends of the saints. Indeed, modern man's imagination is in danger of being overfed: novels, daily papers, magazines, cinemas, television. . . . But it has a still more exciting and certainly more healthy outlet in the endless perspectives opened up by scientific discoveries. The Crusades did much to create a new humanity, more enterprising and already eager for freedom; the voyages and great discoveries of the late fifteenth century helped to awaken a new man, fascinated by his own powers, the man of the Renaissance; and modern man is the grandson of the voyages, enterprises, researches and achievements of the nineteenth century. We can hardly doubt that a new humanity will be born of the inventions and discoveries of today. Wide horizons open before modern man. For him, the attraction of the Church will lie not in miracu-

[1]*Chronicle of Nestor*: in the translation of L. Léger, Paris, 1884, p. 90.

lous hagiography or ceremonial splendour, but far more
in the truth he finds in her of the spiritual relationship
of communion with others—a relationship founded on
the genuine and exacting Gospel attitude of living faith,
inward obedience, true prayer, love and service. God's
beacons on the threshold of the atomic age are Thérèse
of Lisieux, Charles de Foucauld, the Little Brothers and
Little Sisters and their counterparts at Taizé. . . . Our
non-religious age is also the age of a surprising revival
of evangelism. Men want the truth of the Gospel, its
authenticity and simplicity, and on those conditions they
are ready to accept its demands ungrudgingly. We can
no longer hope to dazzle men with purple and gold,
heraldry and titles ending in '-issimus'. He compels us
now to show forth in our lives the truth of what we
profess to believe and love with all our heart.

Who can complain of that?

III

By Way of Conclusion

By Way of Conclusion

I am very conscious of the inadequacy of these few pages in comparison with the holy cause announced in my title. I have been able to approach only from afar, from the outside, and from one particular angle the problem (or rather the mystery) of a Church imbued with the Gospel ideal of poverty. God willing, and granting me courage and strength for the undertaking, I would wish one day to put forward in all humility some reflexions on what is the basis of the biblical attitude of faith, and the very heart of the beatitudes: 'Blessed are the poor in spirit!'

Everything that I have said so far shows that several styles have followed one another in the Church's visible presence in the world. No single formula can exhaust the relations of the spiritual with the temporal; none of the forms taken by these relations fully expresses the reality of a Church whose substance escapes time, being of different order from the things of this world. The Church makes full use of the possibilities that history offers her to live and work in the world; but because she is not of the world she reserves the right to

135

lay aside what has served her for a season, and to use other means or give other expression to her life.

Nowadays she is called upon to find a new style for her presence in the world. A presence founded on prestige, exercising an authority whose superiority was acknowledged even on the level of law, may have been acceptable and indeed required in an age of unanimity in religion. When no other voice but the Church's taught men how they should walk, no other arm but hers upheld them, they accepted her not only as the messenger of Jesus Christ but, within the structure of society on this earth and at the very apex of its social organization, as an authority endowed with privileges, splendour, and the means of action that befitted her station. But now men have taken over the ordering of the affairs of the world and become so engrossed by them that they can no longer find interest for anything else. The world has lost the spiritual unity of ancient Christendom; it is divided, and its divisions are in all probability final. Moreover increased production of the means of comfortable living involves men in such relentless competition, intricate organization, and stimulation of appetites and compulsions that even as they become kings they are in danger of losing the health that was theirs in a less affluent and exalted position.

Confronting this world, or rather surrounded by it, the Church finds herself in a situation which must be recognized not only as one historical situation among others, neither better nor worse than others, but also which conforms much more closely with the law of the Gospel; she is called upon to make a clean break with the old forms of her presence in the world, legacies from the days when she controlled the hand that bore the sceptre, and to find a new style of being present to men. Individual initiative and spearhead groups which have made their appearance in every country have already clearly outlined the shape of this new style; now it must be given recognition, some sort of consecration on the scale of the universal Church, and urged in the strongest terms at the next session of the Council.

I was able to say that the present situation of the Church is in closer conformity with the law of Christian life first, because of the distinction and tension between the Church and the world, which was weakened, if not effaced, by the regime of Christendom. And by the same reasoning, because she has been freed from the dangers of an association or symbiosis with temporal society which tempted the clergy to adopt the attitudes of the world, not to be ashamed to speak the language of the world or to wear the world's tawdry livery of tinsel and gilt. In a world that has become, or has become again, purely 'worldly', the Church finds herself forced, if she would still be anything at all, to be simply the Church, witness to the Gospel and the kingdom of God, through Jesus Christ and in view of him. That is what men need, that is what they expect of her. In fact if we listed all their most valid claims on the Church we should find that they amounted to this: that she be less *of* the world and more *in* the world; that she be simply the Church of Jesus Christ, the conscience of men in the light of the Gospel, but that she be this with her whole heart.

The characteristics of this style of her presence in conformity with the Gospel are outlined in the Acts of the Apostles and the writings of the New Testament. They can be reduced to three terms, compact with the greatest possible spiritual meaning: *Koinonia, Diakonia, Marturia*

(Fellowship, Service, Witness). The World Council of
Churches has made these three terms the foundation, as
it were the tripod on which its programme of action
stands, and by so doing has gone straight to the heart of
truth in its most authentic form. Every initiative inspired
by the Gospel leads instinctively in this direction. The
ground has been so well prepared, so many appeals are
being made to us, that this is the moment for the whole
Church to find the new style of her presence in the
world by establishing, nourishing and inspiring true communities of brothers, projects and associations for service,
and acts of witness.

These three supreme realities could be the starting
point of a positive programme of Christian life in the
world. The demands they make would not only
affect individuals, but the Church herself, *qua* Church,
and hence at the ecclesiological level. These three are
the sure guides to Christian life; but what part have
they in our treatises on the Church? To read them, it
seems as if the Church could very well do without
Christians and without the life of the Gospel?

A positive programme of this kind entails examination
of various forms or attitudes which may in some degree
betray the Church. To be honest, we are often more
sinned against than sinning in our acceptance of these.
We come into an inheritance not lacking in grandeur
and titles of respect, but which is now so archaic, rigid
and ponderous that we risk being incapable of being
to men what men themselves and what the Gospel
require us to be today. In the outward forms we have
inherited from a venerable past we must be ruthless
critics of anything that may on the one hand betray the
spirit of the Gospel, and on the other, of anything that

may isolate us and set up a barrier between us and men. Certain forms of prestige, certain titles or insignia, a certain protocol, certain ways of life and dress, an abstract and pompous vocabulary, are all structures that isolate us, just as there are structures that humiliate or degrade. What was formerly in place in a world much more stable than ours and imbued with respect for established honours is today only a sure way to isolation : a barrier to what we most sincerely desire to express and communicate. Forms designed to inspire respect, to surround us with an aura of mystery, still persist and their effect today is the opposite of what one would wish. Not only do they keep men at a distance from us, they keep us at a distance from men, so that the real world of their life is morally inaccessible to us. This is extremely serious. For it means that we are in fact no longer able to meet men on the ground where they are most themselves, where they express themselves freely, experience their most real sorrows and joys, face their true problems. We are in danger of living in their midst, separated from them by a haze of fiction.

Naturally, our effort should reach down to include spiritual habits or images which themselves depend, at a still deeper level, on the ecclesiology that we profess at least in practice. We are still a long way from reaping the consequences of the rediscovery, which we have all made in principle, of the fact that the whole Church is a single people of God and that she is made up of the faithful as well as the clergy. We have an idea, we feel, implicitly and without admitting it, even unconsciously that the 'Church' is the clergy and that the faithful are only our clients or beneficiaries. This terrible concept has been built into so many of our structures and habits that it seems to be taken for granted and beyond change. It is a betrayal of the truth. A great deal still remains to be done to declericalize our conception of the Church (without, of course, jeopardizing her hierarchical structure), and to put the clergy back where they truly belong, in the place of member-servants. Much remains to be done before we can pass from the simple moral plane where as individuals we act in the spirit of humility and service, albeit within structures of caste and privilege, to the plane of ecclesiological concepts. According to St Paul, ordained ministers in the Church are the joints or nerves on which the whole of the active body relies for its smooth working (cf. Eph. 4 : 16); their role is 'the perfecting of the saints' (that is, of the faithful) 'for the work of the ministry' which is laid upon us all, whose end is the building up of the Body of Christ (v. 12).

We are still a long way from the goal!

To help us make the readjustments that are needed, to give us better understanding of what is at stake, to point the way to new forms of expression and presence in the world, nothing can be more useful than frank exchange of views between the Church and the world, between the Church and other Christians, and within the Church between clergy and laity, circumference and centre, parish priests and theologians or specialists in the different disciplines that have something to contribute on this problem. It is in discussion that each finds the truth of his existence, it is the pooling of resources that gives the impetus needed to meet all the demands of one's personal convictions. For the Church, as for every one of us, health consists not only in being herself, but in working out in her life the truth of her relationship with others. A Church thus open to free discussion will be a Church of poverty and service too, a Church which has the word of the Gospel to give to men: less *of* the world and more *for* the world!

IV

Our Pastors Speak of the Church of Poverty and Service

PASSAGES FROM THE COUNCIL, THE POPE
AND THE BISHOPS

I

A Church of Service

Far from turning us away from our tasks on earth, our
adherence to Christ in faith, hope and love commits us
wholly to the service of our brethren, in imitation of our
beloved Master who came 'not to be ministered unto
but to minister'. That is why the Church is made not to
rule, but to serve. 'He hath laid down his life for us; and
we ought to lay down our lives for the brethren.'

> *Message to the world of the Second Vatican
> Council,* 20 October, 1962.

Our endeavour throughout these four years of humble
service—as we understand it, and shall understand it
to the end—has been that of the 'servant of the servants'
of God, who is in very truth the 'Lord and Prince of
Peace' . . .

The Council has watched the sense of unity unfolding
like a flower, spontaneously, and in a way almost un-
expected by most of us: the sense of unity, or rather of
conscious, recognized and welcome attraction towards
Christian brotherhood, which is expressed in the Apostles'

145

Creed by the compelling affirmation of the one holy
Catholic and apostolic Church, made not to rule but to
serve the nations, among whom Christ's design finds an
answer in a yearning which is sincere, even if its extent
and developments are not always entirely understood.

John XXIII, *Christmas Message* 1962.

The lamb led to the slaughter opened not his mouth
before his persecutors; in his death he reveals to us the
secret of true fecundity.

May this law find its response in the hearts of all who
bear responsibility for the rising generation: parents and
teachers and all those who, being vested with authority,
must regard themselves as being at the service of their
brethren. May it be a special invitation, in the harmony
of obedience, brotherly discipline and common aspirations, to all who labour to spread through the world the
light of the Gospel, the reflection of Christ's resurrection.

John XXIII, *Easter Message* 1963.

Just because we have been raised to the highest level
of the hierarchical scale of the power which is at work in
the Church militant, we feel that at the same time we
have been appointed to the most lowly office of servant
of the servants of God. Authority and responsibility,
honour and humility, right and duty, power and love,
are thereby wonderfully united. We are mindful of the
warning of Christ, whose vicar we have been appointed :
'He that is the greater among you, let him become as

the younger; and he that is the leader, as he that serveth'
(Luke 22, 26).

Paul VI, *Homily at his coronation,* 30 June, 1963.

Let us see the Church as *mater amabilis,* a mother to
be loved. If papal primacy were presented to us as meaning first in service, and as the response to the three-fold
question of love Christ put to Peter, it would be a
language that all Christians, and even non-Christians
understand.

Mgr Hakim, Greek-Catholic Archbishop of Galilee
(*Documentation Catholique,* 1963, col. 56, p. 5).

Their ordination has to some extent 'set aside' priests
to exercise an office of public authority in the Christian
community. And as in the Church all authority is
service, they are ordained as 'servants' of their brethren,
the laity: they kindle and sustain your faith, and keep
ever at your disposal the light and strength you have
need of, the Word of Christ and his divine life.

Mgr Huyghe, Bishop of Arras, *Pastoral Letter to
the Laity of his Diocese,* Christmas 1962.

To have authority in the Church does not mean to rule,
but to serve the welfare of the faithful. The Saviour said
of himself: 'The Son of man is not come to be ministered
unto, but to minister and to give his life as a redemption

for many' (Matt. 20 : 28). In the same way the ministry
of priests and bishops does not mean domination, but
service, *ministerium,* as the pope makes clear in his
traditional reference to himself as the Servant of the
Servants of God, *Servus servorum Dei.*

> Cardinal Frings, Archbishop of Cologne, *Lenten
> Pastoral Letter*, 1963.

The first of the Gospel values : authority seen not as
domination, but as *service.* 'I am not come to be
ministered unto, but to *minister!*'—the Lord's words recur again and again in what the Fathers have said at
the Council. But not only a handful of bishops speak thus.
The message of the Council Fathers to the world returned
to it once more and added : *'That is why the Church is
made not to rule, but to serve.'* This expression is Pope
Pius XII's. It is a straight answer to one of the most serious
and frequent accusations levelled by the enemies of the
Church against her power and her wish for dominion
over States and peoples. It is an exacting programme
for her leaders : *to serve their people.*

> Mgr Guerry, Archbishop of Cambrai, *Pastoral
> Letter*, 1963.

2

A Church of Poverty

Confronted by the under-developed countries, the Church presents herself as she is and wants to be: the Church of all men, and in particular the Church of the poor.

> John XXIII, *Message to the world at the opening of the Council*, 11 September, 1962.

We shall not meet the truest and deepest demands of our times, we shall not answer the hope of unity shared by all Christians, if we do no more than make the preaching of the Gospel to the poor one of the many themes of the Council. In fact it is not *a* theme; it is in some measure *the* theme of our Council. If, as has often been repeated here, it is true to say that the aim of this Council is to bring the Church into closer conformity with the truth of the Gospel and to fit her better to meet the problems of our day, we can say that the central theme of this Council is the Church precisely in so far as she is the Church of the poor.

> Cardinal Lercaro, Archbishop of Bologna, *Documentation Catholique*, 3 March, 1963, col. 321, n. 2.

The Church must find again an aspect that has become a little blurred through the centuries: the look of poverty. Remembering that the apostles were no more than humble Galilean fishermen and that the Lord himself was pleased to live in poverty, she will strive to be more completely faithful to this ideal.

> Cardinal Liénart, Bishop of Lille (*Le Monde*, 12-13 May, 1963).

It is essential that the Church, which does not want to be rich, should be set free from the appearance of riches. The Church must appear as she is: the Mother of the poor, whose first care it is to give the bread of the body and the bread of the soul to her children, as John XXIII declared on 11 September, 1962: 'The Church is and wants to be the Church of all, and in particular the Church of the poor.' She must direct those who have the necessities of life to the work of providing for those who still lack them. As bishops, we must keep in the forefront of our Council's preoccupations the problem of preaching the Gospel to the poor, of the apostolate among the workers. The present Council must be the opportunity of asserting this.

> Cardinal Gerlier, Archbishop of Lyons (quoted in *Equipes Enseignantes*, special number, 2e trimestre 1962-1963, p. 89).

As a bishop, I cannot simplify everything overnight, but I must go on asking myself questions about the

clothes that tradition makes me wear in liturgical ceremonies or elsewhere, on the marks of honour paid to me
in the course of offices and in everyday life. . . .

I need hardly say too that I cannot fail to be concerned
with the problem of honorific distinctions in the diocese.
We shall be nominating canons for the next Feast of St
Vaast, but I know that many priests in the diocese look
forward eagerly to the day when the majority of clergy
will be in favour of abandoning a custom that goes back
no further than the nineteenth century and belongs more
to the spirit of the 'world' than to the Spirit of Christ.

As priests, we must face, for example, the problem of
the adornment of our churches. St John Chrysostom
several times sold sacred vessels to succour the poor. . . .
We need not imitate him too literally, but we must not
be too ready to say that nothing is too fine or too costly
for the glory of God, when two men out of three are
dying of hunger.

> Mgr Huyghe, Bishop of Arras, *Documentation
> Catholique*, 3 March, 1963, col. 323-324).

Many bishops have already achieved a greater degree
of poverty and simplicity in their dress. Why not go
further, and apply the Gospel text, 'not gold nor silver'
literally to ourselves in the case of our episcopal insignia,
and have them in base metal? Another real proof of the
spirit of poverty would be the suppression of worldly and
honorific titles bestowed on bishops. Why not give them
back the title which expresses their first characteristic,
fatherhood in the spirit: 'Father'? Did not St Peter say:

'Feed the flock of God ... not as lording over it ...'?
(1 Peter 5: 3.)

Why retain, outside the church, genuflexion as a mark
of special respect? Still other simplifications, in liturgical
ornament, style of life, etc., could be suggested. Certainly nothing is too beautiful for the liturgy, but the
liturgy cannot justify the appearance of wealth in personal life.

The Pope recently reminded nuns throughout the
world, shortly before the Council (7 July, 1962), that
poverty is not easily reconciled with 'ostentation in
buildings or furnishings which have in some cases given
rise to unfavourable comment'. Why do not missions and
dioceses take more care to keep their buildings, and
especially their living quarters, down to a reasonable
standard of comfort without over-refinement or extrava-
gance? Progressive bishops have gone to the length of
electing to live in humble accommodation in poor
districts and converting their episcopal palaces into
schools. It would be well if their example proved con-
tagious!

Modern business equipment is essential if the over-
whelming tasks of the apostolate are to be more speedily
performed, and this includes bank accounts. But here
again there is immense scope for the spirit of poverty;
for example, if it is a question of transport, make the
choice of a good working car, and never, whatever the
rank to be upheld, of a de luxe model!

The Second Vatican Council is the first to meet when
the Church is already poor, without temporal State,
without political power for her papacy, but more radiant
and more highly regarded than ever before. *Should not
the body of bishops take the initiative by stripping itself*

voluntarily of all that still remains of external signs of wealth, of the temporal power that is now happily a thing of the past? Nothing would bring home to the world more effectively the true nature of the kingdom and the Church. What *spiritual benefits* would the Holy Spirit not pour out on the whole Church if she made herself thus 'poor in spirit', in conformity with the first Beatitude!

From actual poverty thus regained would flow a humility that would make her infinitely more responsive to the motions of the Holy Spirit, more open to approaches for unity, more receptive to the suffering of the world, and more generous in the service of the poor and of peace among men.

> Mgr Mercier, Bishop of Laghouat (quoted in *Equipes Enseignantes*, special number, 2e trimestre 1962-1963, pp. 89-90).

'The Church and the poor: everywhere there is something to be done to make the Church really the church of all, and in particular the Church of the poor ...' Poverty is a matter of life and death for the Church; without it she will lose the world of the workers. For the serious thing is that the working-class population, especially in some regions of Western Europe, is escaping the Church. Those who are seeking the solution in this direction have my whole-hearted support. If anything is decided I shall be the first to put it into effect, to sacrifice what little I have. What is needed is a renewal of the Spirit, not of the Church moved by the Holy Spirit, but of men of the Church ... who are not all saints. I implore

God's grace and blessing for the good of the Church and the people.

> Mgr Maximos, Melchite Patriarch of Antioch (quoted in *Equipes Enseignantes*, p. 87).

The various external signs and ceremonies which enhance the person of the bishop in particular made their appearance only during the course of the Church's history, more especially in the time of the Emperor Constantine, when the external honours to which the high officials of the Roman Empire might lay claim were specified and extended to the bishops. It is possible for the Church to conceive of herself without these external honorific distinctions. Where she faces persecution she must renounce them, and that does no harm to her inner life.

> Cardinal Frings, Archbishop of Cologne, *Lenten Pastoral Letter*, 1963.

The second of the Gospel values: *poverty and simplicity*. How many in the masses reproach the Church for her apparent wealth, the pomp of her ceremonies, her outward show, the place she seems to give to honours, money and 'class' even in acts of worship! This is a real obstacle to the evangelization of the poor and the working masses who feel there is no place for them in the Church. In some parishes in France a real effort has begun to show the Church in her true aspect, poor and deprived in spite of appearances. But there is still much to be done in this direction. Moving appeals for poverty and simplicity have been made in the assemblies of the

Council. They have been whole-heartedly echoed by the bishops. The Holy Father himself, in his allocution of 11 September, said: 'Confronted by the under-developed countries, the Church presents herself as she is and wants to be: the Church of all men, and in particular the Church of the poor.' And the message of the Fathers in Council declared: 'Our solicitude reaches out to the humblest, the poorest, the weakest. Like Christ, we are moved with compassion at the sight of the multitude suffering in hunger, misery and ignorance.' Consideration is being given to the creation of a permanent secretariat to study the great human and social problems, in particular the problems of the poor.

The third of the Gospel values: *the supremacy of love* over legalism in the Church. Too much emphasis on legalism, the result of seeing the Church above all as a society, risks making the obedience of the faithful to the 'laws' of the Church into something purely external, passive and material. People go to mass on Sunday because the 'laws' of the Church require it. They do not know why the Church requires it. They do not know that the Church requires it so that their souls may receive life. Laws are needed in every society, but the great law of the Gospel is the law of charity. The Church certainly is a juridical society, but she is also and above all a community of love. Her inner law is the law of the Holy Spirit, says St Thomas, the Holy Spirit, the soul of the Mystical Body which is the Church, the Spirit of love who fills our hearts with charity; this law must be the life of all the Church's institutions.

> Mgr Guerry, Archbishop of Cambrai, *Pastoral Letter*, 1963.

How difficult it is for us poor bishops of the Church of Christ in the twentieth century to put across the message which at its beginning was steeped in the poverty of the incarnation, the manger, the cross, preached by a working man who lived his life of poverty without even a hole like the foxes, who washed the bare feet of the men he called his 'friends', who used the familiar image of the lost groat. Today this message must go out to men living the bleak life of the proletariat, sixty-five per cent of them hungry, some existing in favellas, slums and shanty-towns; who call each other 'comrade' and are accustomed to the incisive, direct speech of their leaders, to the sober lines of their sky-scrapers, their jet aircraft, and the shorts which are the review uniform of their generals. And we for our part have to deliver this message from the height of our marble altars and episcopal 'palaces', in the incomprehensible baroque idiom of our pontifical masses, with their strange mitred ballet, in the still stranger circumlocutions of our ecclesiastical language; and we go out to meet our people clad in purple, in a car of the latest model or a first-class railway carriage, and our people come to us calling us 'Your Eminence', and genuflecting to kiss the stone of our ring!

It is not easy to struggle free of all this weight of history and tradition.

> Mgr Juan Jose Iriarte, Bishop of Reconquista (Argentina) (*Le Monde*, 1 June, 1963).

Because the Church is a form of Christ's presence in the world, she must reproduce Christ's image as per-

fectly as possible, and in her visible as well as her hidden
life.[1] The poverty which is the sign of the Incarnation
must be the sign of the Church too.

All through history, customs have crept in, in ecclesiastical usage as well as in divine worship, which are
inspired by worldly vanity rather than the simplicity and
brotherhood of the Gospel. We have good grounds for
thinking that the Council will in this sphere meet the
aspirations of many of the clergy and the faithful. ...
Already, for instance, the Fathers have adopted the
principle of allowing no privileges to money in liturgical
ceremonies, which should mean that the classes come
together at funerals and marriages.

But here again, no reform can really bear fruit if
Christians as a whole do not resolutely and whole-
heartedly enter into the spirit which inspired it.

In short, the Church will find her true style of living,
and will be the Church of the poor, only in the degree
to which every Christian strives to live by Christ and,
like him, to be 'poor in spirit'.

Mgr Guyot, Bishop of Coutances and Avranches,
Lenten Pastoral Letter, 1963, p. 16.

[1] Cf. Encyclical *Mystici Corporis*, ed. CTS, pp. 24-5.